Thirsty Scholars

A celebration of Hulme People

Tina Cribbin (Author)
Anne Finnegan (Design/Edit)
Abigail Finch (Illustration)

First published in 2019

EMPIRE PUBLICATIONS
1 Newton Street, Manchester M1 1HW

ISBN: 978190936070-9

Printed in Great Britain.

Contents

Acknowledgements 7
Tina Cribbin 9
Donegal Frank 19
Anne Finnegan 25
Tracie Daly 37
Phil Lukes 45
Marie Finnegan 57
Lorna Orr 63
Jimmy Lennon 67
Frank Agar 71
Roy Bennett 81
Joe Tierney 93
Jem Calame 103
Harold Pursehouse 111
Alison Forbes 115
Sally Casey 121
Hazel Bedford 133
Brian Roberts 141
'The Hopton Hopefuls' - A play by Tina Cribbin 149

This book was created and organised by the Top of The World project which is run by "the beating heart of Hulme" Anne Finnegan, Tina Cribbin, Hazel Bedford, Christopher Finnegan and the great Sally Casey. We have also been joined by artist Abigail Finch who did the beautiful portraits of the community. The book was derived through all the stories being shared in the old laundry room at Hopton Court. We felt it was important that we honour those voices in the community and that these were accessible and shared.

The book is free to community organisations and a free online copy is available.

Acknowledgements

GRATEFUL THANKS TO Hulme and Moss Side Age Friendly Board, One Manchester Housing Trust and Manchester City Council Neighbourhood Investment Fund. Without which this would have not been possible. Thanks to Karen Ward on the Greenhey's Facebook Page and the great Tony Kelso and Manchester City Council archives where we have used some images.

I have had the absolute honour of interviewing and transcribing this book. It's been quite a journey I have laughed and cried but above all been immensely proud. It has only reinforced to me how truly special our community is! The greatest thing about Hulme are the people! In the face of adversity our true colours shine through. And what colour! Rainbows, mosaics, carnival paint, glitter; banners all come to mind as well the black white and every shade and culture in between.

This is why we should honour our heritage and keep fighting for what makes Hulme great! A special thank you to all those interviewed who gave their time and stories so generously.

Tina Cribbin 2019

This book is dedicated to all Hulme people and to Harold Pursehouse and Brian Roberts who sadly passed away during the making of this book.

Tina Cribbin

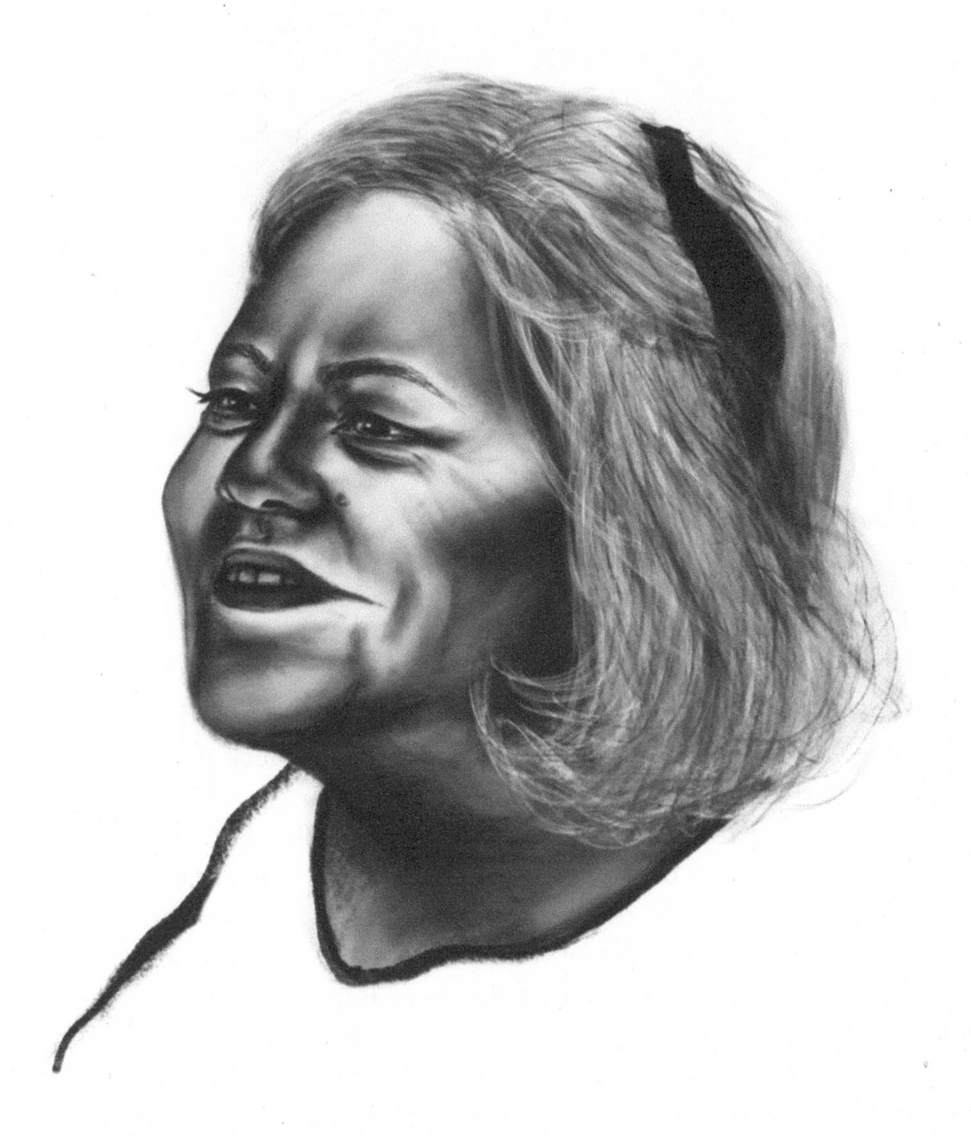

I HAVE TO THANK Bridget Halliday for this pictured which was discovered in the Hulme Sweet Hulme project. (Check out the fringe! That's my sister hairdressing skills!)

I was born in the old St Mary's next to the Ritz nightclub. I remember my mam telling me about how they were all fagging it out the windows on the ward all ready to give birth. I suspect this was an omen because I spent a lot of time in the Ritz fagging it as well!

When I was born we lived in rooms in Ripon Street in Moss Side like many of the Irish community. We moved into Hulme Walk at the beginning of 1971, the year our Noel was born as he came straight from Hospital to there with no electric. My mum sent the older ones to the chippy. The rooms were lit by candles. We had no electric for four days until my mum found out she hadn't actually switched it on!

I clearly remember how big the flat felt and how I got lost in the box room upstairs. I knew like most my mum was really happy that we moved to somewhere nice. I have plenty of memories playing on the landings, in the lifts, the subways and playing in the broken down Ear Hospital

My happiest memories as an adult in Hulme are around the Top of the World project headed by our own Hulmeites, Tracie Daly and Phil Lukes, who brought Hulme to the theatres of Manchester and London!

Some of the cast from "can you hear me from up here?" we had just finished performing at Home theatre.

I've capture some of my older memories in this poem which I hope says it all about how I feel.

Concrete! Concrete! Concrete!

Burning shimmering dusty concrete
the balconies the crescents the walkways
Concrete to climb on, jump on.
Fall down on, grit indented on knees.

Tribes of kids running and screaming on dried out patches
Of hard core grass that refused to give up.

On good days, life dictated by your next adventure,
Under the crescents play scheme,
Or over the bridge park.

Up at the crack of dawn, already dressed..
Nearly out the door, Then I hear her.
Oi! All the belly!
You can get me messages before you
Go off gallivanting with yourself.
A ham shank and a bottle of Sterra!

Of I run down the balcony,
Heart beating fast,
I'm going faster than the six million dollar man!
Run down three steps..
Jump down five…
I'm dreaming of that tyre swing!

Here you are mam,
I'm at the door...

Madam Falang you can take your sister with you!
Gutted!
I stomp down the landing with our Mandy shrieking behind me.

Get down the stairs,
Sneak a quick glance up at the flat she's there,
So I bend down all concerned like,
And say to our Mandy if you button it
You can have some of me blackjacks.
But I don't swear just in case me mam can lip read.

A backing track made up
"Save all your kisses for me"
Whilst our Liz forced me to learn
The dance routine even though I hated it!

Gangs of catholic kids
Attending the evangelical Sunday school.
Which provided a great free babysitting service,
For when the mothers were nursing a head.

Mothers shouting from three floors up
Chanting a list of their kids names
And if you were out of hearing range
Some kid would find you
"Your mam's shouting. You're well in for it!"

Mumbling old men and dads
Muted in the background
Tobacco stained brown

The women loud brash survivors,
Battle faced,
Faced life head on, with a smile,
Sometimes brittle
Or fragile
But always there just the same.
Irish Kath in her later years. Still laughing

My mam Irish Kath,
Mother by day, party girl by night,
Packs of American tan tights size XL,
Ten park drive and a bottle of Guinness for me blood.
On special nights, pan stick and cherry B.

Little Margaret,
Big Margaret and
Singing Esther with her bright red beehive hair
That didn't move an inch in the most legendary of her fights.

You could work out time and what type of night she had
As she left Hulme labour club with sound of Esther's Argument
Followed by a song
And then the sound of her cork platforms
Clonking unsteadily towards the chippy

As I lay next to our Caroline
In the big bed
With the window wide open
And the heat wrapping me into a dream like state

New Hulme

Old voices faded
Echoes like the concrete
Blasted or crumbling into oblivion.
To make way for the new builds,
New faces
And a sense of respectability
That didn't sit comfortably with those left behind.
The diehards
Those who still wanted bicarbonate of soda and boiling bacon
In the shops where they now only sell hummus and kale.

We're just a community of ghosts love, he said
We're just a community of ghosts
These invisible souls drifting amongst us
Like air, like light,
Like their almost too frightened to take
Up this tiny pinhole of space
That as a community we've allowed them.

But these men
They worked brick by brick
Stone by stone
Pint by pint worked with all their might
Hod carrying back fingers crack hard like steel.

Young boys with men's jobs
Earning a few bob
Sending it all home to a land of make believe,

So they worked and they worked
But how they suffered for this land
Eyes became bleary hearts became weary
Quieter and quieter they grew

Until suddenly they aren't big men
They sit and think back when, well when my life was.
But if you listen carefully you can still hear the gentlest whisper
And sense the tiniest tremor
Beneath their Celtic heartbeats
Of dreams of passion
Of a grand old tale that might just happen

I see you, you and you
The sparks, sharp edges unspoken pledges
Winning and losing
Loving and leaving
Wearing your heart like a road map
Of just dreaming dreaming dreaming

You boys your still warriors

And now the dust has settled in Hulme
We begin to hear a heartbeat returning.
You will see some of our tribe shaking down their feathers
Peeking out behind the new apartments and university buildings.

We recognise each other we have part concrete in our veins
Which gives us strength, knowledge and determination
To come together
To rise and fly like only a true Hulmite can.

We are here to RECLAIM!
In order to have a community that shares
We need a community that cares.
We need our spaces filled
With the old the new temporary or just visiting.

Filled with the legends.
The believers,
Dreamers,
The thinkers and the solitary figures.
Hulme was and still is a home to ALL.
Inclusive, risk taking and forever changing.

A place that inspires and captures your heart like
the softest rainfall

Donegal Frank

FRANK HAD NO INTEREST in my photography skills or my interviews skills!

I persisted because this fella is a true legend of the block. He once told me and Anne that he remembered in the war having black flour because of the shortages. It was black because it was made with bits of the bog. We said" what did you do with that?" he said "we made black bread". We asked "what did that taste like?" He said "chocolate"...with a glint in his eye.

Frank Is originally from a small rural village in Donegal moved to England in the 1950s Frank is a long term resident of Hulme. He is also our resident Seanchai, a storyteller who holds tales of Irish culture and heritage. At the sessions, we wait with baited breath for the next pearl of a story to drop from his lips.

I came to England in 1956 I was 19 years old when I got on the ferry.

I first arrived in Glasgow wanting to work on the building sites but came in the Scottish two-week break for whit. I found myself a job working on a farm picking rhubarb and other seasonal products.

I then went to work on the sites for a while followed by a time when I worked as a charge hand digging tunnels where I laid the charges before the explosions needed to break the land. It was difficult as I was so far down that they had to be careful due to air compression. I recall a time when a friend of mine who didn't come up quick enough was found with blood coming from his ears and later died. There was no safety equipment them days.

Happiest memories

"The fields covered in violets as far as the eye can see, I can still smell them"

"I remember I was about nine or ten and went out rabbit hunting in the night in the fields and the woods it was fabulous, we had them for dinner the next day"

Happiest memories now:

"Well, being with the group at the drop-in having the craic, going out to places I look forward to it lifts me up for the whole week knowing I've got that you see, but the best trip by far was the canal trip when Anne made Irish stew and we laughed and sang Irish songs, great times. I want to go again!"

Frank with the lovely talented Christopher Finnegan

Here is a little taste of what we are delighted to hear from him each week

The Shortcut by Frank Carlin

I'm happy enough now though, well, you have to make the best of it. No I'm happy with a wee drink, my radio, the races, the fags - my little pleasures are important now. I don't get many visitors but I do have my pals, my Hopton family. I was a big man back in the day I worked hard and danced and drank harder.

Now the only thing I have to offer beside my dashing good looks is a tale. I've been told I've been kissed by the blarney stone and have the gift of the gab. Well now if I was an Englishman they would say I'm clever. But that's another story. Now, let me tell you an Irishman will tell you a story like he is making love to a beautiful woman and I must say I do have a glad eye for the ladies.

Now then… it was a beautiful summers day in the hills of Wicklow. I was visiting a friend of mine. I got off the bus and wandered into a wood to what I thought was a short cut to the village. Anyways the wood was shaded but every now and then you catch a glimpse of sun streaming through the rich emerald trees making shadows that danced. The light and smells of the wood seduced you into a dreamlike state, nothing could make this moment finer except a drop of the black stuff to quench my thirst. Well now, in any case and anyways I carried further on and came to a sort of clearing with a blanket of the most beautiful, beautiful, flowers; violets they were, shimmering in the sun. In the middle was a big old tree gnarled and knotty like myself but its branches were softly swaying showing its soft light green leaves. It was magical alright, just then I noticed a little girl, a beautiful Irish girl of about 5 or 6yrs old with auburn ringlets, freckles and a white petticoat. She was bending down picking some flowers and smiling. Behind her was a tall slender lady with a beautiful long black cloak and an air of sadness surrounding her? She reached out her hand to the girl and the little girl turned to look at her and just then I knew I was witnessing something truly beautiful, the little girl turned and the woman's face blossomed into one of joy and pure happiness.

Just then a mist began to form and the two of them became more and more ghostlike then they just disappeared into the mist that began drifting off leaving only a small breeze which sounded like the banshees songs of yearning in the woods.

I rubbed my eyes. Now then, did I imagine that? I've not had a drink! Jaysus what was that? Anyways and anyhow in any case I carried on with my journey. I came to a small stream at the edge of the village just before the green. There, sat beside the stream in an old bench, was a couple chatting and chewing the fat. But still I sensed they were waiting for something I sensed they had waited a long time.

I went up to them "how are yer? Do you know where the ale house is, I've a terrible thirst on me." The man looked up and said "well fella you look like you've had a funny turn, sit yerself down a moment". The woman turned in her old tweed coat and paisley scarf, her eyes filled with tears as she said to me.

"Stranger have you by chance just come from the wood?"

"Aye" I say.

"Did you see them?"

"Yes I saw a beautiful child and a woman I think was her mother. But before we could speak the mist came…"

She held my hand and said "I have not seen my daughter for twenty years and my granddaughter for twenty-five. My granddaughter went playing in the wood when the mist came, my daughter grieved something terrible and spent her days wandering the woods, finally the mist came and took her as well. But every year at the same time the mist allows us a visit through a messenger. Today it was you, thank you my heart is gladdened to know they're still together". With that they stood up linking each other and pointed to the old white ale house.

It was hard to make out what had just happened but I tell you one thing, there's always magic when you're in old Ireland. Now, my glass is thirsty!

Anne Finnegan

ANNE FINNEGAN "the beating heart of Hulme" is someone who epitomises the saying "going above and beyond the call of duty". Anne has her own very successful "AFTS" Anne Finnegan Theatre School which has been running for thirty years. She also runs the 'On Top the World Project' and the over-fifties group at Aquarius. Anne was also central to the play "Can You Hear Me From Up Here" where she supported residents on a huge journey and performed!

Anne cannot ever do enough for the people of Hulme and always works above what is expected of her. She tirelessly advocates on behalf of older, vulnerable people. As well as giving her time to cancer charities such as Maggie's cancer support centre Manchester and Teenage Cancer Trust where she has worked with a number of stars, including Rick Astley!

Performing in London

Hulme Girl

I came to Hulme when I was five or six, I came with my twin brother and my little baby sister. We moved into this big house and I remember looking at the two rooms and all the big windows. The big window in the living room was huge to me. The floor was all brown tiles but it all just seemed so big and the pavements were all cinders. They had mapped the pavements out but they hadn't yet been laid. So cinders were everywhere and the houses were all brand spanking new. I remember it being a really feel good time for my Mum and Dad and it was just a new forest for me to explore. I remember standing at the corner of the three houses on our block watching a little rich girl that lived across the way; well I thought she was rich because she had a three wheeler bike. I used to look at her with her bike and posh dresses and white shoes. I wanted to be her friend because I wanted a go of her bike! It took me about three days to go and speak to her and then we were friends until we were young adults really.

St Augustine's School

I went to St Augustine's, I walked to school every morning and walked home. Mostly everybody that I knew went to St Augustine's I think it was an okay school and it had a diverse group of children coming through its doors. It had a church next door which we used to go to and I used to love singing the hymns, Oh yes I loved them. I have a twin so we were a bit special. Robert had a chorister's voice so whenever there was anything going on in mass or a celebration the choristers would be up and I would be prancing on the altar.

We always played outside Pauline Moor's house and we used to play ball or hopscotch or if there were two good lamp posts we would tie a rope so we would always have a swing around the lamppost and we would nearly garrotte ourselves at least ten times a day on this! Outside the flats where the bins were there was an incline where they let the bins roll down. I was never allowed rollerskates because my Mum couldn't afford them but Pauline had some so we used to take it in turns to roll down this incline and then one day she rolled and split open her chin, I was delighted because she didn't want to do rollerskating anymore so I had the skates!

Slightly changed... Capri Ballroom.

I loved dancing from an early age, although I was a late starter. I think there was an advertisement on Piccadilly Radio my Mum and Dad always had it on. It was for the Capri Ballroom on Platt Lane offering dance tuition.

Did you know initially above every Co-op building was a ballroom for health and well being

One Saturday morning my Dad took me down to the bus stop next to the Dental Hospital and he took me to Platt Lane, that walk seemed so long! And then I stood outside the big brown doors of this big building and there were stone steps and inside an old fashioned swirling bannister and I could hear piano music and I got brought in they were having a Tap class - I couldn't believe it! I could hear all these tap sounds. I refused to go home. I just kept saying to my dad 'no I want to stay' I think I was about nine then. And that was the Linda Cardwell School of Dancing, that was the beginning of my dance career. They also had a big ballroom and we used to sneak in and hide underneath the chairs peeking out watching all the ladies swirling around in their beautiful sticky out dresses. To me it was just a beautiful world of sparkly dresses and ladies who were so elegant when they danced, it just used to take me somewhere else.

The New Ardri

And then I had to get a bus home and run past the Ardri because that road was so dark. I would ring our house and let it ring 3 times then dad knew that was the signal I was coming home and to come and meet me off the bus. Sometimes he didn't get there on time and I would leg it past the night club.

High School

Well I nearly passed my eleven plus, I remember my head master saying I had failed by one mark. So my brother and I went to St Pius, the uniform was so hot and horrible. I was only there until the Christmas exams and when I returned they put me in all the higher streams. I was devastated because none of my friends were there. I got bullied like crazy by them. After that I got moved to the grammar school but my mother was going mad because she had to buy another uniform! Then about three months after that everything went to the comprehensive system! At St Pius I remember having my first love there - Joe Casserly and he put 'I love you' on a dinner ticket and put it through the fence.

Teenage Kicks

Growing up I was a disco Diva for definite - some soul and new romantic; Bryan Ferry, Roxy Music, Human League and Adam and the Ants but I loved all the Manchester tunes as well. We used to go to St Edwards on a Sunday night in Rusholme that was great!

I used to go the Air Cadets because my brother was part of the Air Cadets and so was my fella Brooky and we used to go to the discos there and we thought we were dead grown up where they used to decorate the hall with the parachutes. I remember on a Friday night most of the lads round our way went and they all had uniforms, I think it gave the boys some behaviour fabric and we used to hear them marching home. They used to drill on the way home about ten or fifteen of them.

My Mum and Dad would go to Hulme Labour Club on a Friday night and they would think we would be all sitting in the house watching telly. Well every single window in the house was wide open and every single kid that we knew in Hulme was in our garden and the music would be blaring it was a crazy place and what we would do is to put somebody on watch and they would be watching down to Bibby's Ice Cream Van for my Mum and Dad coming down because that was a three minute walk but in those three minutes we would close every window turn the music off, get rid of everybody and dive into bed as if nothing had happened, that was every Friday night.

Around that time there was Aquarius and Proctors youth clubs, but I was always at dancing classes, my brothers and sister were more involved. I did think then it was still very community orientated. All the Mums and Dads knew each other, all the women supported each other. So there would be shared food and childcare if you were locked out someone would give you a bit of dinner till your Mam got back. If you were seen to be naughty or someone was causing trouble with you, neighbours would check on you. It was a big community you felt safe and loved – there was a camaraderie. All the kids that you grew up with would all meet up and go clubbing and all walk back home by Oxford Road, there would be about twenty of us walking home and we never got a bus because we were so close we could walk, because my Mum and Dad were very involved in Hulme Labour Club there was always stuff going on there.

Events such as the kids' disco, the Christmas parties and the Queen's

Hulme Labour Club

Jubilee wow! That was massive! There was a massive outside party. Outside our house used to be a huge car park which is now built on. But that day it was full of tables of food and I remember us being on a float. I remember my mother running along the side of it shaking her Union jack flags. My Dad wasn't too happy, her being an Irish woman an all. You never felt out of it, you could just join in with whatever was going on.

Hulme Changes

I remember a lot of people moving out and a lot of my Mum's friends, people I grew up with, had left and moved out to Wythenshawe up that side and it seemed to be then that a bit of the sparkle went, that togetherness went away. And the families that were left had to gather themselves up again because it was fractured. I remember my mum felt she lost a lot of her friends, it was a tough time.

On Top Of The World group trip to the canal

Hulme Now

I am involved in the community by mistake! But, I am involved because I want to be involved and because I can't not be involved because Hulme is where I come from and if you can give back you give back. I love it. I am involved with the On Top Of The World Project and working with the over 50s in Hulme; if I make a difference to one person's life or make somebody feel that they are important and needed, that's enough for me.

I think the under belly of Hulme is still strong, there are still some people who are original to the area and some new. Community still exists, we just need some more glue. I feel things are improving, there is strength building because we are engaging and working hard and making people feel important and valued and letting them feel its okay for us to be who we are. We deserve to be treated with respect and feel wanted and important. I think because of what we are doing I get a sense that people are a little bit happier. I still feel though that the community is somewhat fragmented in that there are some groups that are happier within themselves rather than integrating into our community. They say they want to but the rhetoric and language don't say that. It says 'yes we want to live in Hulme but this patch is for us'. Those people have had education, that doesn't mean to say people from Hulme don't have education. But coming from this socio-economic background we weren't really told to aspire and because we weren't told we don't believe that we deserve a good education, be eloquent and stand our ground. But I think slowly a lot of Hulme girls and boys who did have education are now standing up and stamping our feet a little bit harder and I think that's what we need to do.

I know that there are people living alone and dying alone in Hulme. I know that the On Top Of the World Project and other projects in the community are trying hard to address this. But there is one thing saying you work in the community and quite another being on the ground knocking on doors, persuading people, making relationships with people and picking up their issues making them feel worthwhile. You need more grass roots agencies on the ground and we need to make those agencies work for us, not the other way around.

I want people who live in Hulme to feel safe and grounded in Hulme so they can live their best life here and never feel ashamed to come from Hulme.

Tracie Daly

TRACIE DALY is undoubtedly Hulme's very own hero. In her role of community engagement officer at the Royal Exchange Theatre she brought a three-year project to Hulme which culminated in the 'Can You Hear Me From Up Here' play. It was selected as one of the finalists for the City Life awards and Manchester Culture Awards in 2019. She brought Hulme to theatres across Manchester and London like a true Hulme girl; confident, challenging, risk-taking with the biggest heart but above all determined to get her community heard. She managed the 'Hulme Sweet Hulme' project with one Manchester and Reel Mcr. She also ensured that the project left a legacy in Hulme which is where the 'Top of the World' project came from. Although Tracie is currently working elsewhere her heart belongs to Hulme and will be back with more exciting community projects. Watch this space!

Duxbury Square

Hulme Then

I was born in Lloyd Street and we moved to Hulme when I was about eight or nine months old. We were absolutely made up to given the flat, it was a ground floor flat in Duxbury Square it was three-bedroomed with a small box room. My parents liked it because it had an upstairs and downstairs toilet, radiators and everything was brand new with lots of space.

My first memory of Hulme is being in the flat in Duxbury Square with my family. Playing and my dad coming home from the pub doing his Elvis impersonations!

One of the best things about living in Hulme as a kid was just playing. It was just one big fantastic adventure. I just remember being out all the time and I mean all the time! We used to play knock a door run across the landing upstairs because there were so many hiding places. There were big families and absolutely loads of kids so we would be all out in the square It was kind of safe because they built these man-made stone structures that looked like little pyramids that were dotted across with one little tree growing out of it. It was a concrete playground. I have such good memories as a kid. We used to play kick the can and it wouldn't just be a few kids playing, you're talking twenty thirty kids each side that would go on for hours and hours! We would also have these wars where we would be all soldiers and nurses and we would fight Arnesby Walk and it would get pretty heated at times.

Holy Name School

Similar to a lot of kids in Hulme, we all went to a school in Moss Side called The Holy Name as it was literally across the field. We could see the school from our flat and we had one small road to cross and even though we were told everyday not to cross, it we did! The majority of us were Irish catholic, I remember all my teachers from primary school. Holy Name really nurtured me as a child because it gave me the opportunity to do my drama and performing arts because I loved it from day one and they made sure there was always room for me to do it. The school made me feel really cared for, it was like a little bubble - it was just lovely. All my teachers stick out for me and I haven't got a bad word to say about any of them. I remember Mrs Blackwell, Mrs Glass, Mrs Grennan but Mr Dillon is the one who stands out for me. There was also Mr Whittle, Mrs Darlington, the caretaker Mr and Mrs Gannon and I even remember the dinner ladies who were amazing.

I remember being about 12/13 years old and the music around then. Well I was brought up on a cocktail of music really because it used to spill out of every window especially in the summer there was such an atmosphere. There used to be a guy called Conrad who lived down the way from us and he loved his music and it would all be soul, and then there was a lot of reggae and lovers rock being played all the time so we all got straight into that. In the early 80s I remember one song that really takes me back to that period is Lisa Lisa and the Cool jam, Baby I am wondering and Soft Cell! Tainted Love. So what we did when all the parents used to the pubs on a Sunday or even a Saturday afternoon we would be able to take over the flat and there would be about fourteen or fifteen kids in the living room and we would all be doing the Adam Ant dance to Prince Charming dancing from one end of the room to the other. I remember that so well!

As a young person I discovered the Contact Theatre that's only because I walked past the building and I heard loads of noise going on. I heard young people so I knocked on the door and asked what's going on, can we come in? So this guy Phil who was running it said come in. I absolutely loved it because it was drama and games and I was blown away. I was there then every week and then they asked me to audition for a main part in a show on the main stage which I got and it was for six weeks it was a Brecht play called "The Resistible Rise of Arturo Ui." They cut my hair off, much to my disgust, and gave me a fringe. I had to be there every night and every single person in that show went on to film and TV. They signed a film star book at the end of it. It was a massive experience for me.

Tough Times for Hulme

At that time there was a side that was amazing and the community spirit was fantastic and everybody knew each other, and everybody was in and out of each other's houses and you felt really safe. But then there was stuff starting to happen where money was really tight and it was hard - it wasn't any strange thing for us to go over to the Post Office or be waiting for a giro to be posted through the door. Or to go over to Aytoun Street with my Dad to sign on and the queues that were there. I remember going to Moss Side Precinct to get these giros cashed. And also around that time there was a lot of problems with the properties, a lot of leaks and it became natural for people just to have buckets, and then the cockroaches started to kick in and they were just getting worse and worse. The decline was rapid and started to be very visible and we were one of the last families to be moved out. All the families were asked to move but because we were on the ground floor we were the last to leave. So basically we lived in the square where it had gone from this really vibrant community full of kids to a sprinkling of families and all the windows being blacked out and silver steel shutters everywhere. It got quite bad really.

So we eventually moved across the road to the estate facing Holy Name Primary School which was on the border of Moss Side and Hulme, I still stayed in Hulme because that's where I belonged and all my friends and family were dotted around. Then about five or six years later I moved back to Hulme with a great struggle because all the properties had been given over to all the people who had moved into the area. It felt like the original Hulme people were not allowed back in.

At the time as well there were lots of things kicking off and Hulme was party central and there was a rave scene which I was part of. Then people moved into Hulme like the Squatters and the Anarchists there were a lot of parties going on, it felt like a bit of a demolition site. We were returning with a huge sense of belonging to the place where other people arrived and it felt like they were just trashing it. It was a strange time and then my son came along and I thought I would pursue the performing arts route because it was the only thing I felt really passionate about. I walked over to Hulme library and saw that they had some drama groups going so I enrolled myself on that. I really enjoyed it and then that was the start of my journey really. I went to college then off to university.

To be honest, even though I loved the content of the course at University I felt like a spare part there, it was a completely different environment for me. There was definitely a class division, I really felt it. We were from different worlds completely even though MY world existed within a three minute radius of that space. But despite this I successfully got my degree and went on to do an MA.

Can You Hear Me From Up Here

There was a project already happening with One Manchester and the Royal Exchange. So when I became their Community Engagement Officer I really wanted to take the lead on that project because Hulme was in my heart and I felt I could be the person to go into that community because I knew it so well and could make it happen. In some respects I already knew the characters and the issues and I knew what I wanted to do and support people to make stuff happen. I also knew that I wasn't going away until I had made that happen.

Thoughts of Hulme

It's a funny time in Hulme right now. I think if you are originally from there you carry quite a strong accent and you carry quite strong characteristics of the place where you grew up, so you know hardship.

You know the barriers to making a success of yourself when you come from that background and that is something that will always stay with you. The older I get the more I realise what Hulme people went through which was something quite profound during that time. It was Europe's biggest social housing disaster and there is something about that period that never leaves you. Although we went through some kind of social housing experiment things weren't all bad. People were looking in and calling us a ghetto but actually there were people from all walks of life of colour, creed and diversity living quite harmoniously together. So when I stepped out of Hulme and moved further afield like Oldham where there was segregation and communities didn't exist harmoniously I was really taken back by that. I had never experienced that and I was shocked.

Hulme Now

I think there is a very strong influx of middle class people coming into the area co-existing with the pre-existing community and there are borders starting to pop up and it feels like there is a claiming of the land and people who have the resources to make that happen are carving out a little village for themselves among the development. I feel the pre-existing community have been very let down and continue to be let down by the powers that be and that they have been forgotten. I also think people are really getting fed up of it now and are ready to fight back.

I also want to say that people talk about the work they are doing in Hulme with people but I would say look at the older blocks; people are dying in there alone and then you will see how much work needs to be done.

I wish that the pre-existing community, I mean those of the last generation and those who returned after the last development, stood up for themselves and claimed back a bit of their space.

Phil Lukes

A TRUE HULME LAD who was not only raised here; he also continues to work in the community. After varied roles in Hulme he is now the Cultural Lead of One Manchester. Phil works tirelessly supporting community groups and individuals. He was central to bringing Hulme to the theatre with the "Can You Hear Me?" play. Phil is a very talented musician and songwriter. Phil is simply our community legend.

I was born in St Marys and my first memories of Hulme are when it was the terraced houses with props supporting them. We lived at Avenham Street which was just off York Street which went right down to the then York/Aaben but my favourite name for it was the Unit4 cinemas.

Our side of the street was completely propped up because it was at the time of slum clearance, they were sending everyone out to places like Partington, Ramsbottom and Hattersley. I have snatched memories of just being on the street and I remember the doctor giving me a kind of chrome robot which I suppose he got from one of his reps, I was made up with it. I remember pushing it through the letterbox then being crestfallen when I found it on the step in pieces. I also remember being tied to a lamppost by Pete, my older brother, who tied me with his cagoule by putting it on me backwards with the hood over my face! He found things like that hilarious. He will still be laughing when he reads this!

So from there we moved to Bentley House and Humanby Avenue. My brother Pete was still up to his tricks, whether it was an encyclopaedia being thrown or a bucket of water when you walked through the door. He did that kind of things for years! I remember in my twenties I was playing football for a team called AC Hulme which was set up by Bridget in the then what was Clopton Walk shops and the old bank (formerly Williams & Glynns!) I did some creative stuff and football.

★

I remember we were playing a team who were top of the division then and there was a big centre back called Clifford Andrew who used to live in the flat above us in Humamby Avenue, when we were playing the game every time he came near me he would kick lumps out of me. I remember saying to him 'what's going on?' and he said 'that's for all the eggs you threw at me'. It wasn't me, it was my brother - every time he would walk in and out of the passage way my brother would egg him and my brother would go 'Phil! Phil! Come out here' and I would go to the little balcony to see him throw eggs at Clifford and when he looked up my brother would duck and I would be there! He was actually fine once I explained everything.

I went to St Wilfrid's Nursery and St Wilfrid's primary. I remember we moved to Stretford when I was just turning eight and I still stayed on at the school in Hulme, my dad had his electrician business in Cornbrook so he used to just drop me off every day. But he would drop me off really early every morning. So I would get to school for about eight o clock. Then I would walk over to the shops to get a few sweets spending ages deciding which ones in McColls thinking I've only got 10 pence and I was supposed to have saved at least two pence for the bus! But most of the time I went to my Aunty Marys next to the school so it was fine.

Those streets near Humamby were great, we had Leaf Street Park,

I still remember those old sweets....so this picture is for Phil!

and there was a walkway that connected Humanby and Humberstone Avenue which we called the hovel. It was a great space for football with a very large goal where we would play centring and heading there was loads of us. They were like play streets because where all the front gardens are now, that used to be pavement. So we used to play with the Turners, also my Aunty Mary had four girls and we were five boys so we were just in and out of each other pockets. The pinnacle for me was the field where we'd go come rain or shine it's now called Letsby Avenue and is like a small woodland area and we'd swarm all over it in endless games of football, of course we would use the 'No Ball Games' sign as a goal post.

Some great characters who I remember were "The Frightening Old Ladies". I remember going out of the block which was fine because I was going to play but returning going in the dark when the two old ladies were there was frightening. Looking at it from this end of the telescope they were lovely old ladies who were mightily fed up of all the balls being thrown against their windows!

Another old lady, Mrs Robinson, lived near us - she was also lovely. When our Pete used to babysit us on a weekend when me mam and dad went out and the meter ran out, Mrs Robinson would always provide us with the two bob needed then my mum would sort her out.

Where the waste ground was next to Proctus Youth Centre is where we put our bonfires weirdly as did the other avenue so there was a great rivalry and you would have to have people guarding them! And they would build them with gaps in so you could sit inside. And all that going round collecting wood in a big pram stacked up precariously When you think back now, how lethal.

After leaving St Wilfrid's I went to Stretford Grammar School even though I moved schools I still associated with Hulme as my connections, friends and family were still there. So my world was still Hulme. Sometimes when I go back to Stretford I walk up Edge Lane especially in the summer. I remember saving my bus fare to get a JUBBLY! I remember they lasted hours and seemed enormous and I would sucking them until my lips bled and when Nationwide came on the telly.

It was a funny time for Hulme; it was changing and I was always at Loxford Boys Club and then suddenly someone says "come to the adventure playground" and suddenly you were like where has this come from? A fully formed fantastically dangerous wooden playground and I never noticed it being built! It put ping-pong at the boys club in the shade! I mean my holidays from the age of 5-15 were whit week at Prestatyn in Wales camping with Loxford Boys Club, we all lived for them holidays. My dad volunteered as a cook and as well as my two uncles and brothers as they got older they became staff in the camp. So we didn't bother with family holidays.

When I was in 8, in Junior 2, our form teacher was Welsh. There

Me and Pete in the Loxford camp field on what was a really muddy year. I think I'm wearing my oldest brother Dave's denim jacket.

Loxford Boys Club

were about 5 of us going to camp and she made us promise to bring back a "Welsh word". I was obviously the only one listening, so one day as we walked down the road called Ffordd Penrhwylfa towards Dyserth and Cwm I spotted my Welsh word and filed it away for next week at school. After registration on Monday, Miss Cameron asked, "Well boys, did you bring me back a Welsh Word". Smythie, the Hoyle twins and the others all looked blank so I put my hand up. "Cul-de-sac" I said… I was laughed out of the room when she told us it was French!

Loxford Boys Club

Yeah so during my first years at high school I still gravitated towards Hulme, especially North Hulme Adventure, Leaf Street baths, then going to the chippy over the bridge faced with that tough choice - Fanta or a bag of chips?

I remember from being very young I was always into art. I went to South Trafford College to do art but I didn't do as well as I wanted to. I think because I also found music when I was drafted into my Brother Chris's band back in Hulme. The previous bass player left after trying to brain him with his guitar! Yes, our famous band was called THE DOZERS! We played covers and the odd song of our own, including a really terrible one that I wrote called "Every Roman Nose" which earned me the nickname Phil Forty-Chords as there was a chord for every word of the song! I got better though; stuck with it and now I'm in a band called Dislocation Dance, and we still perform a song I wrote about my childhood in Hunmanby, called "What Can The Matter Be?" after the song we used to sing about those poor (scary) old ladies, Mrs Shenton and Mrs O'Neil.

It was written in 1995 but I didn't record it until 2005 as it suited their album "Cromer":

Mother cooks lunch on Sunday
Eat your greens there's no bread today
Fathers sizzle in the oven
Likes his gravy good and bakes on

Oh dear what can the matter be
Have you got your toast for playtime
Leave it on the pipes it tastes like
It could still be half past eight
You'd be smiling at your plate

Granny wants to take a photo
You won't stand still you don't want to
Mother waves her fist in your face
Caught on camera, fixed in a frame
You say "oh dear what can the matter be?"

The "Granny wants to take a photo ..." verse is about this picture. I don't know why I didn't want my picture taken but it got snapped just as my mum waved her fist at me. She hated it and ripped it apart. You can just see her fist! The other half is in my dear old dead gran's collection

Someone is calling me, what can the matter be?
Mother is running well this can't be right
(She chased me home for tea)

To the Doctors; on the way home
Eating chocolates from a paper cone
Uncle John he always claims his
Auntie's in the Belgian navy say
"Oh dear what can the matter be?"
(This is a really beautiful song)

This was around the time when Thatcher said there was no such thing as society and top sliced a lot of the services which has not been rectified really.

Hulme then and Now

There are remnants still about, especially around the Aquarius community centre, and the parts that didn't get knocked down in the 90s. I came back to Hulme in 1982 and shared a flat with my brother, we lived on the side of St Wilfrid's and that was the hub, the church social club and there were pubs then, you know.

Later I went to work in the Hulme project that was based in Otterburn Close they basically knocked two flats together and put different agencies working together such as architects, Direct Works and housing to solve the problems of Hulme. I remember the first day starting there and I turned up to be told that I had to report to personnel in the Town hall I didn't actually realise I worked for the council, I thought it was just a well-meaning project!

The job I do now is amazing, we started initially working with The Royal Exchange in 2013 with the Booth Centre and once that was finished we started working with what became The Top of the World project. I love the job because it allows me to build relationships with people and organisations which create change

Hulme has always been home to different communities but despite that or because of it Hulme is very community minded and I think it needs to be. People need each other, the times that we have been through in the last ten years of austerity. If there is a plus side to any of it is that the community is growing stronger. What we are trying to do is get people joined up together to make the community stronger. Hulme has always been amazing in finding creative solutions to how they live, and how they get on and how they get on together. Hulme is simply amazing really.

If I had one philosophy in life I suppose it would be to try your best to spread a little happiness.

Marie Finnegan

An Unsung Hero

Marie has been actively involved in the community for many years working in many places such as Hulme tenants and residents and Saint Wilfrid's food bank.

St Wilfrid's Church

Marie has been doing something beautiful in our community since 1999; she has been giving communion to the sick and elderly. She has worked all around the estate as far as Chorlton-on-Medlock. "I have to say that I got more out of it then they did," she says, "honestly they were some amazing people who also wanted just to chat and have someone beside them when they were at their lowest I suppose. However, it was an honour."

Marie has also volunteered at an "out there" group that was based at St Wilfrid's set up by the daughters of charity. They offered support to wives, husbands and children of prisoners. Her role was to accept calls from the helpline and manage the office. "People just needed advice or someone to talk to so they did not feel so alone," she says. Marie volunteered here for four years part time among all her other work in the community.

Living in Hulme

When Hulme was bombed in the war we were moved to Wythenshawe, it was a beautiful garden city with one small hangar at the airport! Then I moved to Alexander Park and back again to Linbeck Cresent in Hulme but finally settled in Hulme in the 1970s where we lived in Otterburn Close. It's strange that the new age travellers came and they got a lot of really bad press, yes you get them in the van some playing music but honestly it was a place that became iconic, I saw a picture that Tony Kelso put of them abseiling down the close I saw all my Jimmy's cars at the bottom.

Otterburn Close

Otterburn Close

They integrated with the families and the families just got on with it. I mean I used to see it on the television this place called Hulme - they said it was a no go area and no one could go out as it was too frightening and I thought what are they talking about? I could go out at any hour and feel safe. I used to get the bus at 5am - I might not feel safe now.

But some of the characters at that time: singing Esther, Margaret Wilson, big Kath - all the women were great but we had to be strong and get on with it. We just had no choice. A lot of the men were laid off and times were tough. The only way they got work was vans would come and say "right we need so many".

There was a drinking culture in Hulme and life was shaped around pub hours for some, and you could find more than beer in the pub, you could buy things cheaper like meat, so you know you do what had to do.

The gas explosion in Hulme: The story of Gwen

"Fire crews battled for an hour-and-a-half to rescue Mrs Gwen Harding from the rubble of her fourth-floor home in Hulme, Manchester, after it was demolished in an explosion that shattered windows and shook buildings over a wide area.

"British Gas investigators at the scene said vandals had snapped a gas pipe in the flat underneath Mrs Harding's in the six-storey block and a build-up of gas had apparently exploded.

"The injured woman, who lived alone, was said to be ``poorly but stable" in the Manchester Royal Infirmary last night with 30% burns and leg injuries." (The Herald 1996)

There was a lady Gwen who was a lovely lady, she lived on Bonsall Street and if you ever met a lady with such a poorly chest it was her. Then I heard that there was a fire; how she survived that I do not know. She went into hospital for a very long time and she was what you called a character, she didn't take fools gladly and she put people in their place but all them new age travellers who had such a bad press collected money and made sure that it got to her. A lot of them came to see her in hospital and made sure she got anything she needed. And even after she moved here they found out where she was and they came to see her then she became a celebrity! She would sit there and say such and such is coming to see me tomorrow.

I spoke to a policeman who said how that woman survived with such injuries, with her age and her bad chest. Well it was a miracle and she did survive. Eventually she began to forget and her family placed her in a beautiful home and I used to go and visit her. Even then she forgot a lot of things but she never forgot the fire and she still thought she was a celebrity there! She was a character - beautiful and hilarious.

Hulme now

There isn't a community now. Those old flats were crawling with bugs but you know what, everybody knew, people helped each other out and I feel like we are this little dot in the middle of university land now. I don't know if anyone else feels like this but I feel we are not really wanted, we are tolerated. I think the final aim is for the University to buy all the land. Personally I don't have a problem with the students at all but it's the powers that be making decisions without proper consultation. For example the science park sent me a letter about it but it's actually a done deal and a PR exercise.

My philosophy on life:

Be happy with what you've got but don't put up with things that are not right, make your voice heard. I love those who are doing work in the community like Aquarius and people like yourself but I feel tired now and think you have a big job ahead. And I really do believe that the University should be doing so much more.

Lorna Orr

I MET LORNA at Aquarius over fifties exercise class. I was immediately drawn to her cheeky laugh and mischievous face. She looked like a warrior who walked all over the rules written down for her. I wasn't wrong!

Early Days

I have lived in Hulme for over 50 years. I came from Jamaica when I was 13 years old. I left my friends and family, well my grandparents who I was very close to and they brought me up really because my mum and dad were already here. I didn't like Manchester at first, the weather, the houses, it was congested!

When I came I went to South Central high school it was near where the Junction pub is. My first day of school was horrible I found a lot of racism there which I was not used to. It was mainly white children then. But it was the Irish and Jamaican children that were targeted with name calling and, I would say in a racist way. All my friends in school were Irish and I think it was because we were both going through the same difficulties. The other thing that surprised me was that the education I was getting back home was better. When I came to England my learning went backwards instead of forwards.

At that time I was living in Fulton Street off Alexander Road near where all the shops. That row had everything: fishmongers, butchers, a Post Office and the GP was there as well. Like most people then, everyone shared the house. The house we were living in belonged to a member of my family. She was related to my dad so it was comfy there, so it was us, my aunty, uncle and my mum and dad. There was only one person there who wasn't related but they were like family, to this day they are like family. I saw her yesterday and she is in her 80s now.

Work

When I left school I got an office job paying £4 a week, then I got offered a factory job at £5 a week so I took it! I was expecting to get five pound in there but I only got four pound 12 and 6 after national insurance and tax, so I took it back to them and said "this is not right I'm supposed to get five pounds!" The woman looked at me like I was crazy and said "you have to pay tax and insurance" but I didn't know anything about that then. I was so mad. Everyone left and I said I'm not leaving until I get my five pound. The supervisor in the end said "ok I will give you the five pounds but you must give it me back next week". I said "I'm not giving it back next week!" In the factory we made ladies knicker boxers.

That factory was somewhere in Moss Side near Denmark Road. I wasn't there for long because I didn't like it. So I went back to the

Great Universal Stores

office job, the one I left before the supervisor said "you were the best person for the job why did you leave? We have just employed someone this morning." I said "can't you tell her not to come" she said "no we can't do that." So I said "send me a letter if anything comes up." I went home very upset that day. So I said to my dad "I need a type writer to practice on to keep up my speed on my typing". So he said "I can't afford to pay for one out right so go to Mr Neflor and ask him to order it out of the catalogue" so that's what I did. It came in a little case. It was very good and I had it for many, many years and at some point I got a job at this place typing letters to the courts that led me to another job to do with the catalogue in Ardwick at Great Universal Stores (GUS) where we did admin and sorted out people paying the bills, it was in an office block connected to it.

Working at GUS in Ardwick was my happiest time. I was there for quite a few years.

Going out

I wasn't allowed out, no way! And if I did go out I had to lie and sneak out - well I just went to house parties and things like that. Listening to soul and reggae beats. I remember one night I crept upstairs, the light was on so I went to my bedroom and I jumped into my bed fully dressed. The next thing my mum came in and I did feel her! I asked what's that for? She said "where you coming from?" I think she was worried about boys! But she needn't have worried - every time I went out my cousin Courtney always looked out for me and made sure I got home safe.

I was 22 when I got married and I can remember meeting him for the first time! I had more than butterflies! It was he who spotted me at first and he had his eye on me. He knew my cousin Courtney but he didn't know we were cousins and he thought that there was something going on with my cousin. And my cousin protecting me didn't make him any the wiser.

Looking back

I mean there were good times and bad times - racism was rampant and you felt you had to watch your back all the time. I think the racism I experienced just made me stronger and more determined. I remember even when the riots were on and there was little money and no jobs people in the community were quite caring.

Now

I think it's much better now because people are more accepting of each other, I live in Stretford now but I still do keep in touch with Hulme my friends are here, for me it's just the same I still have all my family friends and connections here. Hulme to me feels just like going home. I like Aquarius I've been coming for a number of years.

Jimmy Lennon

A much loved, larger than life character in our block. It's safe to say that the drop-in wouldn't be the same without his smiling face and dulcet tones. It was difficult to get an interview with Jimmy as he spent a lot of his time posing for pictures.

WELL MY FIRST JOB was down the mine. I was 15, in Bellshill, Scotland. My job was to look after the ponies - I didn't have a choice whether I wanted the job or not. You had to work and that was it. I worked six hours a day down there but what I really wanted to do was drive a big lorry all over the country, just to be by myself and enjoy life.

My best job was in demolition - breaking stuff! I was eighteen years old, I even had my trademark moustache then! Now I take each day at

Burt Reynolds arrived for the drop in

a time and hope I last as long as my mother who died recently aged 98. Her name was Mrs Mary McAvoy, she liked to sit at the window. She was a tall lady. She had her curlers in and bright red lipstick every time she went out. She did had a lot to say for herself after having eleven children, two to her first husband who died, then nine to her second.

My mammy always bailed me out, even though I was considered the black sheep of the family. I remember her saying "behave yourself and grow up!" I still haven't though (he smiles through his moustache).

Jimmy enjoying a quiet one with the lovely John Sullivan "The Quiet Man"

Frank Agar

GENTLEMAN FRANK has been a resident of Hulme for most of his life. He is known for always being a gentleman and a sharp dresser! Frank has worked all his life for Manchester City Council initially as a painter and decorator, then as a charge hand.

Frank is a walking history book and a true story teller who has introduced me to the world of Johnny two rivers and Charabancs but more of that later.

"I was born at number 11 Pickering Street, Hulme in 1947. I just remember being happy riding my tricycle at 5 years of age and my dad teaching me to ride on a two wheeler. We had a long lobby, the parlour was all posh done out in lino and it was saved for best and the rent man! Then at the back was the kitchen. My favourite memory is sitting in our long lobby on the steps reading the Beano or Dandy on a Saturday morning listening to the sound of the rain.

"My neighbour, who also lived on Pickering Street, was Joseph

Frank enjoying the day out in Skipton with the young Christopher Finnegan in his Irish guards outfit which he found at Skipton market. He changed clothes and went back in the pub much to the delight of the fellas and Frank who nearly fell off his chair.

Rigg. He had about six or seven kids but this man actually wrote the poem about the Munich disaster. I don't know how he got to be a poet but obviously this poem got published.

"What we found out after researching this was written by a Joseph Rigg who was a boxer and piano player in Hulme and it's an actual song that he played in the pubs of Hulme, it has been published somewhere and we have contacted Manchester United Museum for them to have a look."

TO THEM BY J RIGG

Pause for a while, and a tale I'll relate
Of a team that we justly had to call great
A long time may pass e're we see such a team
For Busby just skimmed all the top from the cream

In England and Europe, yes world football too
These youngsters knew precisely what to do
No bragging or boasting
The best! The rest will remember their name
Remember them well and hour them too:
Reflect on the glory they brought home to you
Bryne, Jones and Colman, Taylor, Whelan, Pegg, Bent
How could they have known their short lives had spent?

Crickmer and Curry, Bert Whalley the gent
Who'd work day and night a defeat to prevent
Can you forget them? Well brother just try
And brush away that tear from your eye

The good Lord above must have made a decree
"I need them in heaven for eternity"
And somewhere above they now watch as they say
"Onward United let none bid you nay"

No matter for now, what the future may hold
Your exploits are legion, UNITED THE BOLD
The world shall remember (as each of us do)
The greatest team ever - the team that was you
And some day, perhaps, on the Old Trafford Ground,
If we listen with care we may hear a strange sound
As from up in the clouds with pride you look down
And see 'The Babes' wearing your own triple crown.

BILLY TWO RIVERS

I remember I must have been about 10yrs old when my Uncle Joe went and asked them if the lad could sit here and they said "yeah it's alright". I was in the Russell club, my dad left me upstairs with the wrestlers who were playing pool, there was a long bar at the back. Well Billy Two Rivers was very famous then. And he asked me to put chalk on his cue.

Well that's my claim to fame!

Billy Two Rivers also went in the Crown pub with his son, and also he wrestled in the Labour club.

There were some great characters for example Mitzy Moore and Hellcat Hagerty.

In fact when I was painting and decorating I was winding up Mitzy and Hellcat and they were having none of it and Mitzy picked me up, all 14 stone of me and threatened to throw me over the balconies.

Hellcat Hegarty

After speaking with Frank I was surprised to find out that Hulme was an area well known for wrestlers!

CHARABANC
(Manc: SHARABANG)

Factory day outings (annual works trips) in the 19th and early 20th century were quite common for workers, especially for those from the northern mill towns of Lancashire and Yorkshire during the wakes weeks. The 1940s and 1950s were relatively hard times due to national recovery being slow after the Second World War; rationing was still evident and annual holidays had not really become established for poorer workers such as weavers and spinners, so a day's outing to the seaside was a rare treat and all that some workers with large families could afford. "Charabanc trips" were usually only for adults, again due to finance. Occasionally the mill owner would help to pay for these outings, but this was not always the case.

It seems all over Hulme 'Sharabangs' were grand days out from the pub leaving early morning to Blackpool or Southport, as the old bus would leave, nothing would be heard apparently apart from the sound of the pouring of beer for the long journey…

HMS Illustrious

Two mates, their dads and the HMS Illustrious aircraft carrier

Having a beer in your local is nothing new but like Brian says it's a weird coincidence as they didn't know each before moving to Hulme.

It just so happened that they were talking about the war and Frank mentioned to Brian that his dad was at sea as did Brian and his dad. Frank mentioned the name of the ship and Brian goes "that's the same ship my dad worked on in the war". They found out that their dads worked on the same ship throughout the duration of the war. What a coincidence. Even stranger, Frank brings into the pub a picture of the crew of HMS Illustrious and Frank pointed out his father and to the shock of Brian there was the face of his father as well!

Frank's dad, Able Seaman Wilfrid Agar, worked on the decks pulling the chocks away from the Swordfish fighter planes while Brian's dad, Able Seaman John Kenny, worked below in the engines.

Frank's Dad

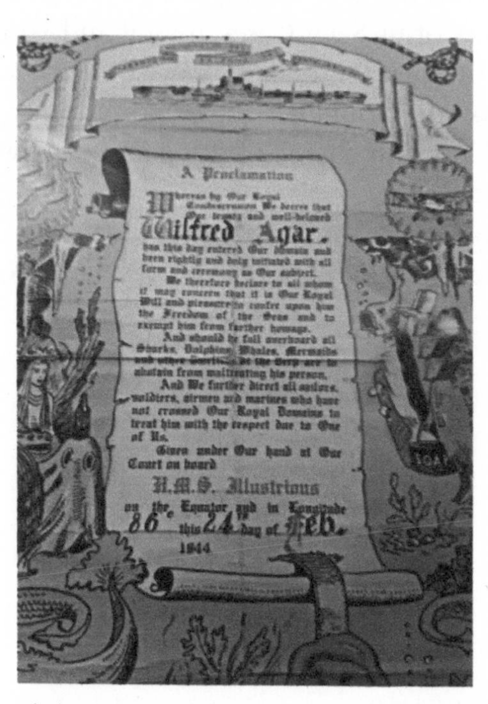

When they crossed the equator they got their hair chopped and shaved then they got dunked. But they also got this diploma for crossing it.

Frank (right) with Brian on our day trip on the canal boat.

I've had good times and bad times, well it was rough about twenty years ago but you don't tend to remember those times. Well we've got good neighbours now, but although there's still a sense of community but once the likes of us Sally Casey, myself and yourself go there will be nobody left. It's just for students now that are only here for three years. Before this you would get all the community information from one of the pubs but now there's nothing and now we only hear about people who died.

My philosophy is "keep it simple". All these kids now are under pressure at school get a job, get a house. It's hard these days.

Roy Bennett

Roy (first left) on our trip to Transport Museum

Growing Up

I WAS BORN IN HULME on 8th October 1954 in Vine Street off Stretford Road not far off the Golden Eagle pub that everyone called the Nudger, because you always got someone nudging you for a bit of money or a pint!

My first memory was how big the old terraced housing was; we had a massive cellar. And every time it was my birthday or Christmas from 5 onwards I would ask for parts of Scalextric and I built a massive track there and I had it until I was about 13 until I sold it. Those were such great times.

At the back of Vine Street there was a big grass area, that's where everyone played and where all the bonfires were and where all the kids birthday parties were; we all knew everyone because everybody grew

Roy (right) having a brew at the drop-in with Jimmy.

up with each other. It was safe; all the kids played cowboys and Indians, they were great times and I miss them very much… very much.

We moved from there in 1965 as it was being demolished and they wanted more people in the area then. When you look at town now and how built up it is, yet in the 60s when they built cities in the sky everyone was having a go at them.

I went to Webster Street School, the old one where they had the playground on the roof. I can remember some near misses! There used to be a playground on the roof at City Road School as well, and Epping Walk Park above the garages.

Webster Street School

It was good at Webster and I left there in 1964 because my dad wouldn't let me go to a bigger school in Hulme, he could see how things were going. So I went to Openshaw Technical High School and in the third year that got closed down when we joined up with Newton Heath High School and moved to Moston Brook. I enjoyed high school, I just loved sport so it was football, rugby and all sorts. And I did sports at home.

Epping Walk Park

I went to Proctors Youth Club they had a junior club, which I think was 4 til 6pm, then it was the older kids but you had everything; you had a gym, table tennis, weight-lifting room, and there was a boxing club there. So for kids nowadays; we didn't have computers, phones or anything like that but we were out all the time. We used to play football at Birley High School probably 6 nights a week. And my Dad would come over two or three times when it got to eight o'clock and say "get home".

We didn't want to sit in the house, it was great time; there were loads of places to go to. Leaf Street Baths for one - I mean it was a disgusting place, there was moss on the walls and God knows what else! You had a little park next to it and in later years it became known as Spider Park.

There were loads of shops about as well on Alexandra Road and you could get anything in the sports shops on Princess Road.

Proctors Youth Club

Birley High School

First Job

My first job was as an apprentice painter and decorator for a company called Arnold Sharracks who were based in Rochdale. After a while with them I went to Salford College to learn the trade, things like marbling; the wages were £3 15 shillings a week, that was in about 1969/70 and the lads I used to knock about with were working in the warehouse at Dunlops and coming out with £20/£25 a week so at weekends they would say "we are doing so and so and are you coming to the football" but I couldn't on my wages because I had to give me mam £2 for keep. Most of the time I was there I worked on Cross Lane in Salford. I was there for about ten months then this lad came up and said to me "someone has been sacked at the warehouse, all you will be doing is carrying the loads of cloth" well I thought £22 a week isn't bad at sixteen! I regret it now though. But saying that I hate painting now! I didn't like it at school. I preferred Maths, English, History and Geography. I don't particularly remember wanting to do anything specific when I was younger. I just think I was one of those kids that would take whatever came along. I had a few jobs; I worked in Dunlops for a time, how could anyone do 12 hour shifts in there! Then I was at Carmacs on Cambridge Street, that wasn't very nice.

First Pint

I went in my first pub when I was fifteen and half, and I started to grow a bit of a beard at fifteen and we'd been playing football on Birley High and we come back and there were a couple of bigger lads there who were the same age so we snuck in the Nudger and went in a corner. We all ordered Watney's Red Barrel and a bag of crisps, the girl behind the bar served us no problem. We caused no trouble and made no noise but this woman kept staring at me, so I started staring back - I didn't realise who she was. She went out and about fifteen minutes later my Dad came in and he gives me a right going over. "Get out! Get out!" he starts shouting and as he's walking out he turned and said to her something like "mind your own business". I never went back in a pub until I was 18!

The Grants

The first pub I used to go in then was The Grants, there was a good set of lads in there, a good atmosphere - I mean the pubs we had then were numerous: The Grants, The Crown, The Falstaff, The Grey Parrot, and that's just on the Jackson Street side. Then you had The Unicorn, The Mancunian. In Clopton Walk you had a chip shop, hardware shop, a supermarket, a butchers, a chemist, a greengrocers, a lady's hairdressers, a bookies and a bank. We couldn't ask for anything more. It was a real community. I mean going shopping you would be talking to everyone telling you so and so has done this, and have you seen our lad he didn't come home last night. Everybody knew what was going on, a lot of people could say its people being nosey but it was just a community.

The White Horse pub

Community

You had characters like Father McMahon. The new St Wilfrid's had a fence round it and if you were walking past and stopped to see who was playing, the collection plate would come through the hole in the fence, shaking in front of you. Oh he was a lad, he was a lad! That's the difference now, you would never see anything like that these days. They were great times.

Working at Manchester Polytechnic

In 1978 I got a job at Manchester Polytechnic. At the time it was run by the city council and I loved it, absolutely loved it. We did two shifts - 7am till 4pm and then a 3pm till 11pm. I was cleaning in the Art and Design building and had to keep the woodwork rooms clean and collect big sacks of wood shavings. Then I was in metalwork, which was alright. I remember there was a tutor who, before the students came in, would let me have a go at glass blowing – that was great! And for the student shows we used to do the security and portering and we had to wear a brown suit with a red collar, a white shirt and red tie and we had to put things on the wall for directions and if anyone was struggling a bit we would help them. I used to love that job. I have to admit there were a few times on the late shift before the tutor would come in I would pull out a drawing board and sneak behind there and have ten minutes! In 1982 they had a student sit in, it lasted about three or four nights and we were on the 3-11pm shift and then we used to go to the All Saints building as security till 6 in the morning. Then in 1984 we all got a letter to say it was being privatised, we had the option to stay but in the meantime I knew there were caretaker jobs going.

Working As a Caretaker in the Crescents

I went on the Thursday for an interview at the town hall and I started the following Monday. On my first day the supervisor came round and told us "this is what you have got to do". At the time in the Crescents there were still a few families remaining but they were all moving out and then there were what we called the Crusties and the caravans. There were a lot of dogs about and therefore a lot of dog mess, it was the first time I had seen a brush that was nearly four foot wide to brush the whole of the landing on William Kent and the supervisor showed us how to clean between the pebbles on these raised beds. On the ground floor of William Kent there were garages, then you had the first floor flats, then above that you had the upside down flats where the bedrooms were downstairs. It was alright really until things started to get a little bit rougher, you know muggings. You would come down to work and you would get to know the different sounds such as the difference between a TV coming over the balcony and the sound of say a milk crate and hopefully no bodies.

Every morning there were stolen and burnt out cars in the garages. We used to contact the police and tape it off to not allow anyone in until the police arrived. A lot of kids in the primary school would use it as a short-cut so they had to go in another way. As fewer people were there, it wasn't that it was hard, it just got dirtier, with drugs coming in. The thing with Hulme, especially the bull rings, was it was a perfect place for hiding - in minutes you could be half a mile away on the other side of Hulme! The police hated it but I remember watching a news report that said that muggers were coming from outside the area because it was such an easy place to hide. It's a shame really. They got an award for building the bull rings, it wasn't just the bull rings that were difficult, you could get bits of trouble anywhere else.

Last night of the Crescents

I remember the last night of the bull rings before demolition started - it was superb; they got cranes and put old cars on the roof. The Junction was open till about five in the morning they had a special licence... apparently. They set fires and there were bands on, there was dancing and everything and then the community really began to change. At the time we all thought, well maybe it's for the best. I mean people judged you coming from Hulme. I mean the bus driver used to look at you getting off in "concrete jungle". I am glad the Crescent's have gone and people have good homes.

Hulme Now

When I think of our community now, it's difficult. Where we live in Hopton we have got a good little community, we have people that look after us and take us out and this, that and the other but the University has just taken over. Last week for instance it was open day for new students and the traffic was horrendous but we weren't informed. They're building big hotels where it's only for people who can afford it, as it's really expensive. I think the community, as hard as you try, is more difficult to reach because of all the changes and it seems once the university have got their claws into something, like the new blocks going up on Bonsall Street, they can do exactly as they wish. So you're banging your head against a brick wall. I can't think of the future in Hulme now; they're re-cladding the flats again, it makes me wonder if they will push for those as well. I suppose we have to wait to see what happens with the university.

Joe Tierney

Joe Tierney!!

OUR JOE

The cocky tilt of his hat lets you know he thinks he's all that

Tall

Gangly

Meandering

The bluest crinkly smiling eyes, always in the know and a word to the wise…

He rises each morning at 6am; too big trainers, overcoat, umbrella….Well he always was a good looking fella!

75 and life's a breeze, the only problem he has is with his knees.

A taste for curry on a Friday night, goes down nicely with his long awaited pint,

His woolly jumper worn through on his drinking arm, he has the art of telling stories, always handy with a yarn.

Joe is my good friend, a collector of lost souls, he goes from flat to flat with a smile and a friendly chat.

He holds a joke with all the lonely folk.

He spends his money carefully but gives his time and love generously. A philosopher of old

He sits with me on our hard earned bench, long legs stretching out toward the setting sun.

He states, "when it's all said and done, when it's all said and done

"Life is for living my dear… go on now, get on!"

Tina Cribbin 2017

MY MOTHER DIED when I was only five and I went to live with my grandparents in this cottage in County Clare in a village called Kilfarnore - this was our cottage (above). Oh I remember it well! It was lovely it was, we had all our own grub, we made our own butter and everything was natural, we didn't need to go to the shop; they were hard times but good times. There were no cars in them days, you were lucky if you saw one once a week. Only the priest would have a car or the doctor or something like that. We used to walk to school in them days and in the summertime I used to walk in my bare feet. It was about half an hour's walk away.

This is me in the middle the cheeky chap when I was a lad.

Joe's Famous Family

We used to travel to England every couple of years as we had many relatives over here because my granddad and father played in the Kilfenora Céilí band. My father and grandfather taught many of the younger people and the band is famous all over Ireland. My father was there when they won the All-Ireland finals. There was always music being played at home. We used to travel all over Ireland and England; to London, Birmingham - everywhere in the UK.

The first group of Céilí musicians played in the old schoolhouse in Kilfenora in 1909. A new priest invited local fiddler Michael Slattery to form a band to play at fundraising dances to help clear parish debts and refurbish the church. It was also an opportunity for musicians to play at local houses or cross road dances.

The members of the band changed over the years. Early players included fiddler John Joe Lynch and his sister Brigid McGrath on concertina, Jim Mulqueeney and Austin Tierney on fiddle, and Jim McCormack on flute. For bigger events, local musicians such as Jimmy Leyden (drums) and Pat Madigan (bass) and McCormack augmented the band.

PJ Lynch started re-organising the band in 1953 and they won three "All-Ireland Fleadh Cheoil" titles in a row, in 1954, 1955 and 1956. Thereafter they became extremely busy on the Céilí circuit, travelling and playing all over the country. The busy schedule forced PJ Lynch to step back and his place as manager of the band was taken over by Kitty

My Dad and Grandad

Lennane who also played piano in the band. She retained this position for 40 years.

In the 1960s the band played in England regularly to large crowds at halls in Manchester, Birmingham and London. Things quietened during the 70s and 80s however, due to changes in musical taste. In July 1992 the Kilfenora population gathered to pay tribute to the band as they celebrated their 85th anniversary. The event was broadcast live on RTE radio. Then in 1993 John Lynch, son of PJ, took over as band-leader with the intention of re-entering the competition for the All-Ireland Fleadh Cheoil. This was achieved spectacularly by the band repeating its 1950s feat of winning the All-Ireland 4 years in a row (1993-96).

Working in England

First I went with my grandmother to Kent, then I moved to London. My first job was as a cleaner in a café. I was only sixteen, I was too young to work on the sites then. I had a few jobs like that in the jewellery shops, stoking the boilers for them. Then I went to the building sites. My first wage packet was about twelve pound a week; it was about two pounds for your digs in London then. The thing about London was everyone stuck together in cliques; if you came from Clare you stuck with people from Clare, you know.

But when I came to Manchester I loved it because everybody mixed together and I loved that. There were all the Irish pubs and clubs and all the Irish music it was a great craic. I started working, you know, on the 'lump'. I was what they called a "Long Distancer" then. I went everywhere for work, everywhere. I worked in a camp in Bangor in Wales building a power station for Kennedys; the camp had two thousand men in there, we slept in huts with bunk beds, you know. There was a canteen, a priest and even a cinema - we had everything you wanted there. Ah, it was great. We put all the cables in - there were no machines in them days, we would be pulling huge cables all day.

I worked on an oil rig down south in 1972. They were great times. So, for instance, when I was living in rooms in Norman Road in Rusholme, there was a gang and they would say "there's a job in Peterborough"and I was young you know so I just packed up my gear and off I went and then from there I travelled to Scotland - if there was work in the town you travelled to the town.

When I first went to Newcastle, listen to this, it was the first time I ever saw women drinking in a pub! Them Geordies were great. The first pub I went into there was a fight and we were all thrown out. I thought "well this is a great start" then I felt a big hand on my back and would you believe it, it was a fella from the next village!

In England in '72 they made it the law that you had to pay your stamps, before then we were all on the lump getting good money, you know. But I was a year off from getting my pension.

You see when I came over here I didn't go back for many years. You know once I started in London I was off like thousands of Irishmen at that time. You see when I left I didn't contact anyone and the reason I didn't contact anyone was because I couldn't write. It took my sister 35 years to find me. In them days, not many people had the education, you know.

She tried everything, she checked all the Irish firms in Manchester and they found me through Murphy's contractors. Well I went to Birmingham to meet them and what a welcome I got! Then I went to my father's funeral - it was a huge affair in the village.

Hulme

When I came to Manchester I loved the music. Being brought up with the music, you know all the pubs and clubs and the Ardri - all of them! I loved it. I worked as a doorman in many of them. Wherever you went, everyone knew you and pubs were full.

I used to go up Rusholme way, the Lord Lyon, the Clarence. I used to get knocks at my door at nine in the morning for the pubs like The Falstaff and we used to drink at all hours. We used to go to all the Jamaican places; the Lagos Lagoon, the West Indian Centre and the Sheebeens. We would come out of there and sometimes go straight back to the pub the next day! You know they are just lovely, lovely people. I used to drink in the Iron Duke and the Royce and it was all Irish and Jamaicans, we always had a lovely welcome.

Iron Duke

I have friends now I've known for over 50 years. I remember Paddy Fogharty, my best friend. We lived together in rooms and worked together and I was off working away and he was mad trying to find me wherever he was. Anyway I came back and he says "I have some very bad news for you". I said what. He said "I got married" and I thought he was blagging me! So I say to him "who would marry you no more than someone marry me self!" Oh, that was a great night, a great craic. He died six years ago and I still visit his wife to this day. But that's the hard thing now, everyone I knew from them times has died. It's a sad thing.

Sir Henry Royce

In them days, you see we looked after our own community. If someone died in Ireland, we would have a collection. I remember once this poor man had a suit and a collection for airfare and off he went on the same day. Even the gangers looked after people as well. I will never forget when my wife got ill with the cancer and how they all helped when she was in hospital for four months.

Joe having a little sup!

Hulme Now

I like Hulme but it's not the same. There's not the people out there and there's no pubs or anywhere to socialize. That's why I like what you and Anne are doing. I love the going out on the trips and all that, when we go out I really look forward to that.

Although, I have regrets, if I had my life to live again, I wouldn't change a thing. They said I would be gone by forty and I'm still going strong!

Jem Calame

The Diamond of Hulme

Jem's Mum and Dad

BACK HOME IN JAMAICA I looked after the house and the children. My mum was called Ivy and my dad name was called Uton. There were 18 of us. My mum was a very clever lady, she was a dressmaker she made all our clothes and school uniforms. She used to sew for the community and much more. She had got those skills from my grandmother. So my mum did the sewing and we did all the other things needed to be done in the home. She also taught young girls in the district who wanted to sew or embroider by hand. Sometimes it was hard work but I had a happy childhood. We didn't live in the town, we lived in the country in the parish of Clarendon in a little district called Friendship.

As a little girl I had a lot of responsibility as I was the first girl looking after the ones who came after me. There were 12 boys and 6 girls! Even though there were a lot of us and it was hard my mum's ability to sew meant we were very well dressed for school. I remember the school uniform; a white shirt and a blue pleated skirt. And the boys had a khaki uniform. In the Caribbean then you had to be very smartly dressed for school. And my mum made all our uniforms. She sewed for us and also made my dad's clothes and anyone who wanted anything in the community. She could sew dresses and shirts for men - she didn't need a pattern.

I came to England in 1965 and I went to work in Chadderton on a contract where I worked for a year in a cotton mill. I worked on the bobbins machine and we lived there for a year in hostels like huts on the premises but they were very nice inside we had a television and

Jem's family when younger

everything, everybody got on with each other. In the evening we sat and talked to each other or watched TV.

Some of the girls had family who were living in Moss Side so at weekends we would sneak out to there. I found Moss Side different because it was like England it was alien to us and the cold weather which was hard to get used to. But Moss Side wasn't difficult, you found people from back home and you started making connections. We used to go to The Denmark, the big western, or house parties.

When we snuck out we used to have to come out by the factory door where there's a big gate that was locked at night. The men who were working outside on the night shift used to open the gate and then they would let us back in.

After finishing at the mill after a year, I came to live in Moss Side living on Hartington Street and then I worked in Ancoats in a clothes factory. I used to work in the warehouse there doing stockroom duties.

When I met my husband I lived in Moss Side, then moved to Hulme's in the early 70s when they were clearing out Moss Side. I put my name down for Hulme and I was offered a two-bedroomed flat on Arnott Crescent, they were quite big flats. I worked in another trimming factory working on zips. After a while I got pregnant with my first child. I had three children and hadn't worked for a while then I got a small cleaning job and then they opened up Aquarius at the old Holy Name school with Ron Mitchell.

Jem's children when they were younger

That was in 1973. When it first started it was just a building and he used to get fresh vegetables from the market and deliver them to some of the old people. Then from that it was decided to run a play scheme and me and another lady from Boundary Lane worked there. But before doing that my children attended Martenscroft Primary School on Epping Walk and I used to bake a lot for the school, they really liked it when they had fetes, and I used to help out on trips to the seaside so I began helping out. Then we started a playgroup in Aquarius we had to get social services and a lady from another nursery in to support us in making sure we had all the paperwork. Then all the kids came so my son Richard had come with me as a baby and he learned to walk there, he used to be in his little wooden walker going all over. When he got to nursery he was already advanced in many things because of the playgroup.

They used to have discos at Aquarius, it was really nice and as the years went on we would have the steel band in practising. With the school holidays we would take the kids to the seaside and we would charge them 10p, and some of the kids didn't even have 10p, those trips were amazing.

Then the older kids from the estate started coming in and the kids from schools like Ducie that some of the teachers couldn't handle and the teachers would come with them on a one to one but they wouldn't speak to the teachers but they would tell me. It was nice working there.

From there I began working in 8411, it was a little community centre in Moss Side at the back of the library. I worked in the evening in the café bar. That's where it started for me working with the council - that was about 1981, it was very busy in there with all the kids from Loreto College would come for lunch and they used to say that's the best sandwiches they ever had. I feel I'm drawn to work with people, you work with some really good people and some really bad. But you don't let the bad people cloud your view on life.

My boys went to Birley High School and did quite well. While they were there I was on the parent governors board for a while.

When they closed the precinct, 8411 was put into Birley High School which at that time was run by Adult Education Department 8411 – it was like a big family. I went to Hulme Library café and my friend went to the Greenheys Centre. I used to work in the café on the second floor then we moved downstairs to a bigger space which was when the council came and took it over from Adult Education.

Jem and colleague at Hulme Library Cafe

Jem with her extended family (left) and her sisters (right)

Then I worked in Sports City near Manchester City's ground at the café and I would have people pop up and say "hello what are you doing here?". My daughter used to say "how come you know so many people?" but they remembered me, they used have the gay table tennis tournaments there and the man and women were such lovely, lovely people. I love meeting new people. I remember when Darren Campbell came in to Sport City where they did activities for young people during the summer holidays.

I'm retired now and I enjoy doing keep fit and the art class at Aquarius

Hulme has changed, it's not the same as when we had kids here when everyone knew everybody else and you used to know more people. In the future I would like the community to come together. Now it's like we are in a bubble, they are doing so many things around us and they may ask questions such as 'what do you think' and if you disagree they just do it anyway! It doesn't feel like a community, it feels like there are two separate communities.

It is nice to look at my life now with my children and know that I made difference in people's lives, not just my family but from all the work in the community. It's nice when people say hello and they have a lot of respect for me because of the work I did in the past.

I remember when I said I was leaving Hulme Library and no one would believe me, then one day this lady who worked upstairs came down and said "what am I going to do?" I said "What do you mean?" I was really confused she said "who am I going to talk to?" that kept me going and kept my feet on the ground. She said "I can't say goodbye I will have to leave". I thought wow. I didn't realise that I made such a difference to people who came into contact with me.

[illegible] around. She said 'I can't see goodbye'
[illegible] I didn't realise that I [illegible] a
[illegible] contact with me.

Harold Pursehouse

HAROLD LIVED IN HULME all his life. He was the eldest of ten brothers and sisters and was evacuated to Shropshire in the war aged eleven.

He has great memories of this time on the farm where he says it was hard work but good times, he enjoyed the countryside and clean air, where they produced vegetables. He particularly remembers the farmer's wife making him the absolute best breakfast! And liked how she cooked and fed the American soldiers stationed nearby.

Harold loved it so much he stayed on their after the war until he was 19 and did his national service.

Harold then worked for forty years as a lorry driver for Lawlor's where he was always ready to help people, sometimes he would be found helping families doing a moonlight flit! Or, he would turn up at friends and family with odd bits of furniture that he had come across. At that time things were difficult for many and people appreciated his help.

Harold was one of first residents in the newly built Hopton Court, which was built in the 1960s. He made great friends with his neighbours where he socialised in the Gamecock Pub. Helping people was a trait he carried throughout his life.

One night I was told how a good friend of Harold's passed away and he gave everyone in the pub five pounds so they could get a drink to remember his friend by.

In his later years he was known to frequent the Czech Bar on Booth Street West, where the landlady would make sandwiches for the regulars. Harold always had his veg peeled and prepared in the pan ready for him to cook when he came home. Harold was a proud man who valued his independence.

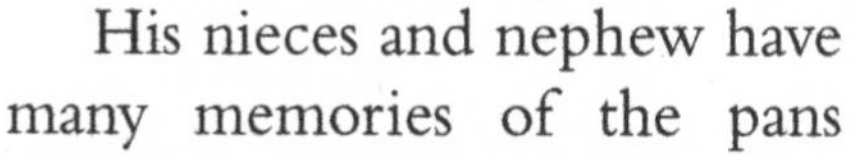

His nieces and nephew have many memories of the pans boiling away. As they do when anyone who visited had to come away with something! Including a few coins he kept on the mantelpiece for visitors.

When Harold became ill and needed support, he was always helping others. He had a good friend in the block called Joe who used to cut Harold's hair when he couldn't get out. One day Joe hears a knock at the door, there was a young lady who was Harold's carer and had been ordered down to Joe with a four pack of Guinness!

Harold would often sit on the bench telling tales of days gone by of what Hulme was like and the characters. He was an important part of Hulme.

He was a great friend, neighbour and a much beloved uncle and brother who will be so sadly missed.

Alison Forbes

Hulme's creative genius! An inspirational woman who teaches us age is just a number! Remember to check out Alison's books which can be found at all good book stores and bought online at Amazon.

I LEFT LONDON and came to Manchester in 1990 because I found London too expensive and I was doing some teaching when I first came up here and the travelling got too much. I taught in a stage school in North London for 15 years. In addition, I taught at the Italia Conti Academy of performing Arts for four years, which was great fun. I loved working with the students and at that time I had a large Edwardian house which I turned into bedsits and rented them to students, which also meant they could not miss ballet, could they?

I moved to Ashton first, while I was there I was still doing some teaching but the travel made it unviable. I was employed in various jobs including selling perfume where I found I was useless. Then I got a job with Group Four securities. I was on duty at the customer services town hall extension when the girls on the desk found an advertisement for a position of residential caretaker. They advised me on the form, I applied, I got the job, and that came with the flat. I was a caretaker in the flats for 15 years and decided to stay on after I retired. The flat has great space and it is so well placed.

I find the longer I am here the more I really appreciate Manchester. It has everything London has but it is far, far more friendly and

Family pic, I'm the little one!

everything is so accessible. I do find Manchester people are really friendly.

When I was caretaking, the council decided that the caretakers have some understanding of law; they had arranged a small course on

Alison receiving her Law Degree

law. I had a friend who was a barrister and I was continually asking questions. In the end, he said "if you are that interested perhaps you should do a law degree" so I did and I graduated at the age of 65.

I found after doing the law degree that I missed writing assignments and that is really what got me into writing a novel. My first book 'Tower Court' is a thriller set in a tower block from the point of view of the caretaker, my fourth book 'Three of a Kind' is a prequel to the others, and it actually starts in the blitz.

I already have five books out, four of which are in the 'Tower Court' series and another one which is a historical thriller set in the 18th century, a Georgian escapade with another waiting to be published.

I was actually born into a very creative family however I was not seen as creative but it all went into dance. I mean I was still teaching ballet in my 50s, which is not recommended, and my creativity had to have an outlet somewhere, hence the writing.

As a child I was brought up in Hertfordshire with mum and my uncle's family - two households living together with two of my cousins who were the same age, both boys. It didn't work out for me because I was the youngest. I was a girl and I wasn't a musical genius. I played a lot by myself. My friend once told me she could not understand my imagination. I had a lot of 'inner life' as it were. I was, and am, very

Alison's books

happy on my own. I live alone but I am definitely not lonely.

What I am looking forward to now is going up in a helicopter! I am going up for my 80th birthday as a present from my daughter. I will

Alison relaxing at home

be flying over Manchester leaving from Barton Airfield. I wanted to do something extra special.

I feel part of the community to some degree. I mean when I was a caretaker I knew nearly everyone in the block and hardly anyone outside and since retiring I know more people outside of the block. I really enjoy my role as cultural ambassador for One Manchester going to the Royal Exchange watching plays it's been amazing. In fact it was at one of these shows when I got talking to a woman who told me about her daughter who was a dance teacher and runs a keep fit class.

Therefore, Sally introduced me to keep fit Anne, and Aquarius, where I attended for about three years.

I found being involved with the 'On Top of the World' project. It was absolutely fascinating and I was astonished to find myself on stage when I swore I would never. I'm happy backstage. It's been great fun and everything that has come from it.

My home is a lovely place and I am thankful to be here. My philosophy on life would be "do not give up and make the best with what you got". If there is anything I would like to do in the future it is to revisit Kenya - it was amazing!

Sally Casey

Her Royal Highness of Hulme Sally Casey

WE LIVED IN Cabra West, Dublin. My mother died when I was 8. There were three younger than me and three older, she was my granny's only daughter and she died at 40 years of age. My gran was permanently grieving for her daughter and then a few years later her son died. How my granny ever reared us I do not know? She must have had steel in her veins. When my mother died the girls were being sent to the convent and the boys to the Christian Brother's School. The day we were due to go, my granny said she could not allow her daughter's children to go. She took us all on at 78 years of age!

When I imagine my granny it would be her sat down, or singing songs or telling us her life story. She used to like to sit in the window and she had a hit on everyone, she would comment "oh yeah I know where she's going and what's she's up to". She had an elastic arm - if you were in trouble her hand could reach around corners to get you! And to save yourself from further punishment you had to let on to die. The roars of you, I'm bleeding! And then she would get scared. But it was total frustration, with managing all those kids. I always remember her coming back from Moore Street weighed down with shopping. My nana was sad but she was good. A good hearted woman!

Holy Communion

We would try to do good things but we had no guidance and we were mad at the world. Our mother had died and I always remember that they didn't allow us contact with her when she was dying. The only contact we got was sitting by the bedroom door listening to nurses and doctors in the room; it was horrible.

Mum and Dad

I remember the neighbour waking me and my sister up and she was crying and I knew what she was crying about. She just said "go in there now and say goodbye to your mammy". When you're eight you want to rail against the world, and there I was being sent into my poor mother who I loved more than all the world, lying there dead. And then that was it, we were sent out of the house at half eight in the morning with my poor mother dead. And they thought they were doing us a favour by protecting us.

The word cancer was an awful word back then and you weren't allowed to tell anyone about it.

Memories of school

I wanted to be a teacher. I was capable of becoming a teacher but because I was a girl, my dad didn't want to know. I loved school. Back then you stayed in the same school until you were 14, there was no high school but I just thrived on learning and I would help the teacher. My teacher was a wonderful human being. I will never forget Miss Collins. I remember her voice and her encouragement. That was about 68 years ago. She was very far-sighted. She knew that us girls should be the best.

Miss Collins was also a singing teacher, she taught us to sing in a choir and I remember we did background noises and quizzes for the radio and we got paid! She was passionate about history and she would take us on field trips. I remember one time she took us to the GPO (General Post Office) where the fighting started in 1916 on O'Connell Street and told us to put our hands on these marble pillars for us to feel for the bullet holes where the English had been shooting. She hated the English and told us all never to go to England!

Sally and her Gran

All my life I have never forgotten that woman, she was amazing.

At 14 I did my big exam, I actually came second in the whole of Ireland. My teacher and my head teacher got together and decided that I could have a scholarship to a teacher training college at 14 if my father would buy my books but my father said no. I knew this was because I was a girl. I knew there was no point pleading with him. He said "No, find a job or better still I will find you one myself!" and he found me a job two days after my 14th birthday in a factory that made sanitary ware for women, picking up cotton from the floor.

You see it wasn't just in my family that girls were expected to keep house.

Sally and Jimmy

Dancing at the Hop!

When I was about 15, I always wore dresses with a underskirts that stuck out and flat pumps and nylons. I used to steal my sister's clothes, I used to eye up her clothes. I loved dancing; Tuesday night was where I met my husband. I mean Cabra West had thousands of people on the estate so you never got to know everyone. You had to be careful at the hop, it was a bit like the Bronx. My husband was 18 with slicked back hair and skin tight jeans and every fella held a comb in his pocket. Jesus, if they only turned sideways and there was a hair out of place, out it would come. And they had little jackets; they were really vain and pristine and if a fella asked you for a dance you'd be afraid to say no in case he gave you a dig or tell his friends you refused him a dance so no one else would dance with you.

I remember I went dancing in Gardner Street in a tenement house where there was no exit, no bar and the sweat would be dripping off of you. My friend lived a couple of doors down and she would bring us a chipped mug of water, there were no glasses. But the music was out of this world, the rock and roll from America. It started at 8 until 10.30 and it cost about a shilling to get in. We would leave that place at night and you would be sweating from your head to your toes, you would be barely able to walk and then I had to walk about two and half miles home. Then you'd take your nylons off, well you needed them for Friday night. You couldn't have ladders in your nylon for a Friday night which was the big night out at a posh place.

My husband was quite quiet in a way but he suited me and I think I needed someone who suited me because me brothers drove me mad. I was afraid of his mother and he had six sisters but it turned out his mother was a lovely woman.

Coming to England

About three or four days before I was due to go to England my father found out and my eldest brother said "Da will be at the boat and he's going to stop you". Even though he had his own life and he never lived with us, my father still had so much power. I knew that if he was there and told me no I wouldn't have gone but luckily he wasn't there.

I was 19 when I first arrived in England. I came on the ferry *The Hibernia* with my boyfriend to live with his sister. My granny had died and I was just so fed up in Dublin and I wanted a fresh start. We got married in August 1963 and in 1964 I gave birth to twins and then in 1967 I had a little girl.

Well, when I first arrived in Manchester, oh my Jesus! I had never seen anything like it. We arrived about five in the morning. We walked out of the station and down the sides of the walls they'd be black with soot. I'd be afraid to touch the walls with my coat, it was horrible and yet looking at them walls I felt happy enough, even in those first few minutes.

My first job was rolling bandages for a Jewish man somewhere near town and rolling these things of cotton wool he was forever coming on to me telling me if I stayed he would put my wages up, well I was on the bare minimum anyway.

Back in Dublin making the sanitary pads in the factory, I was on piece work and the money was good. I used to run all the money clubs in work like the chemist club and the girls would come in with all the make-up. And the shoe shop, then the girls would all come in

with great shoes. If there was an Elvis movie on at the pictures nobody would be doing any work! And you know I worked with them girls in that factory and not once did I hear the word period, it was called 'your others'!

My husband got a job straight away the day we arrived; a fella said meet us in the morning at such and such a place and that was it, he was working for the electricity board laying pipes. Then I went working in Dunlops making Wellington boots and I loved it; the crowd was there, lots of Irish people. Then, Jimmy and I went to live in this little house in Chorlton-on-Medlock. It would be condemned now before you even walked into and then what I thought was a kidney infection was actually the twins!

Hulme then

I remember coming to Hulme in 1969, the twins were 5 and my little girl was two and God, just looking at this house; three big rooms downstairs, three bedrooms and a toilet downstairs - it was like heaven, it was a wonderland. The kids loved it but outside we didn't even have a footpath, it was just cinders everywhere. Hulme was going to be the place to live and it was a happy place. Kids laughing and giggling and then we found St Augustine's, a lovely little school.

A Community Activist emerges

I became very active in school. I started doing voluntary work, then I was doing paid work in the school itself. It started with my neighbour next door having damp and the clothes rotting in the wardrobes. Well, we only had underfloor heating downstairs, nothing upstairs. There was me and about four neighbours and we were giving out stink and we decided we were going to do something about it and over in the community centre a guy said "why don't you get the councillors out" and we called a public meeting because of all the issues; there were mice, cockroaches and damp. On the night of the meeting 109 people turned up, that was in about 1980, so we had been here eleven years but we had suffered and suffered.

And after that meeting we thought we could do something about this, we can have a voice and make demands because then if a tenant went to the housing offices you were treated like scum. There were iron bars across where you talked. This was in the old Moss Side precinct.

We had gone to make demands on our issues and were very, very successful. We would tell the housing that the houses needed families in and they listened to us and did an awful lot of work. Eventually across the whole of the Aquarius estate we got all the problems sorted out and everybody had a warm safe house.

Then we looked at each other and then we said "what about those living in the maisonettes" and then we set on them. The council's initial response was "we have no money" and we said "does that mean you can't manage the estate" then they came back and said "well we will demolish them". We said "Okay but you need to rebuild decent homes for people". We just never took no for an answer and we constantly put pressure on for change. It was hard, we would be having meetings till half ten at night sometimes. There were some people from the city council who were good and worked hard for us.

The old Aquarius was there, it was run by two workers and I was involved in volunteering for a long while. The rent was very expensive and we knew the council would not pay that rent and the church were set to demolish it. After the demolition of the maisonettes we were working closely with the Guinness Trust and were appointed as the builders and they were going to build all these lovely homes.

So we asked them to build a community centre, they said "no our ethos is that we build houses". So we kept asking and asking them, then we said "if you don't build a community centre, all them lovely houses will have their windows smashed because there is nowhere to go and nothing for the kids to do on the estate". That's how we sold it, it would be worth it to you to build a community centre and so they did that but we had to be there at every stage of the consultation which took nine months worth of meetings late at night. I'd be bone tired and nearly falling asleep knowing full well I had to get up at half seven in the morning to get the kids ready for school. Then we were cheeky enough to ask for them to build us a few shops they said "no" we said "go on, you could just put a couple under the flats". We used to persuade Guinness but they were good people. After that we then looked at the high rise blocks and said "we can't have families living in them. The children need a place to play but a lot of people have forgotten what the TARA (the tenants and residents group) did."

Sally meeting Princess Diana

Hulme now

Now I've got many other commitments such as chair of the Age Friendly Hulme and Moss Side Board, Chair of the Top of the World project, secretary of the tenants and residents group, and Chair of Hulme Art group and involvement with the Hulme allotment to name a few! I also volunteer at Top of the World drop-in projects in Hopton Court flats which is mainly single older men. I hope that those people who are involved in the project feel less lonesome and less vulnerable now they know that there's someone they can go to with a problem. I actually feel that the members of that group are looking better within themselves. They are taking care of their own needs. I find it amazing and wonderful to see. I would love to see it rolled out across all the tower blocks. I would also love people to get involved more at Aquarius.

I am quite disappointed with Hulme now, if I didn't love the people here I would be gone. If I had the strength I had in those days I would be out there and I would fight daily to ensure that the university would fulfil the promises made to this community. I'm angry, sad and hurt that fifty years on we haven't got space for our kids to play outside.

In this fight I have with the university I feel I am being ignored. I am being appeased and I'm getting false promises and I don't know how to respond to it all. The university now is a corporate business, it's so large I don't even know who I'm fighting anymore it's just about business and development to them, we mean nothing, we are just minions.

I feel the councillors haven't got the fight or the power to go against them and stand up for us.

My philosophy on life is; have the courage of your convictions.

Hazel Bedford

The True Blue Quiet Storm

Hazel may be the quiet one but she is a driving force in our community and known for her tireless work. I've seen Hazel do untold acts of kindness for people when she thinks no one's looking. It seems that this kindness is a theme that has run throughout her life.

Hazel's Mum

I WOULD SAY the most influential person in my life was my mum because she was widowed at 45 and there were eight of us at home. I was 17 when my dad died and the youngest, the twins, were four years old a week after he died so I see the powerful woman. She wasn't a loud person but she had a quiet strength. You know, I never heard her complain about anything. In addition, she had to deal with compulsory purchase from Ardwick and then we came here to Hulme

My badge of honour

I drew this picture at Aquarius art class, it is of my mum when she was a child.

When we first moved to Hulme, it was so exciting. I remember we came into the kitchen with the sewing machine and made the curtains. That was 1968, I was 20 then. I've lived here nearly 51 years. I didn't know anything about Hulme, it was still being built, there weren't any roads built then. The twins went to Martenscroft, our Graham went to Plant Hill, the first comprehensive.

I was involved in the youth club and was involved in a little group called Plymouth Grove Enterprise where we all donated so much of our wages a week anonymously and we used to do projects; we'd take kids out from the Crescent in Salford and from Longsight and we held Christmas Dinner for years at the church group. I was a Sunday school teacher for several years. It was a beautiful church before they knocked it down; Plymouth Grove Methodist church. It was part of my life for a long time.

I started work at 15 at a warehouse in Trafford Park and I worked there for the best part of 43 years and left when the firm was taken over by Littlewoods.

Me, my sister-in-law and my nephew
Alan and Pauline. 2003

The first time I went to the Etihad Stadium it was quite awesome because I went with my brother and his wife and we sat on the front row. I think the best match was the very first match at the brand new stadium. I had actually been before because I was asked to go because they needed to do the fire checks. So many of us had to go. The very first match was against Barcelona on 23rd August 2003.

I applied to become a season ticket holder and my season card came through when they moved to the Etihad and from the minute you get to the outer perimeter of the stadium we have what you call City Square, so there is always something going on. There's usually groups on or maybe past City players. That's a really good part of it. But I must admit I'm so excited for the game that I want to get into the stadium as fast as I can. I have my routine; I get my chips and a hot chocolate and I go and sit in my seat and wait for the team to walk out and warm up on to the pitch. It's like a ritual and football is a way I bond with my brothers, especially the one who attends, the others are busy working etc.

HAZEL AND CLIFF

Well Manchester City maybe my first love but I would say Cliff Richard is my second! I belonged to his fan club. I have seen him many times. I actually met Cliff at the Apollo. I went to a lot of his Gospel Tear Fund concerts and things like that.

Funny, I have this article when Cliff was 62 which tickles me when he performed at the Arena, he thanked the people of Birmingham! As the papers said, perhaps age was catching up with him! He has gone through a lot in the past few years. Although I feel guilty, I think there's come a time when you need to retire, you know. He still got many fans and I like listening to his music but I do not think I will go to another concert.

Hulme

I didn't make any friends at first because, as I say, I was working full time. I mean even now it surprises me that just joining Aquarius when I retired I started the keep fit, then I helped in the office. Sally Casey says she remembered me by the sound of my heels going to work in the morning. I'm amazed that learning about people round here but I never knew them until a few years ago.

I think we have lost the community because now people want to keep themselves to themselves.

Sally has helped me a lot, she has given me a voice. I have always been quiet. I think she is still helping me be even more vocal. I mean, I do not even know now what my life would be like if I didn't get to know these people. It's opened so many doors that I thought would never be open to me. It's like, now I'm finally getting to know my community. I enjoy my voluntary work at Hopton which is great but my worry is the more you do, the more you're expected to do and now I'm busier than ever!

Well my baseline in life is treat people how you expect to be treated.

Brian Roberts

I ORIGINALLY CAME from Dublin at aged nine, like the rest of the families, we had to move for work. We went to Liverpool and I remember being upset and worried about the new school but you know when we got to Liverpool half of Ireland was there anyway so I didn't get homesick.

My mother influenced me most; she was a Cork woman and she could throw a shoe a mile away and get yer! Arr, she was brutal! There was nine of us. She used to threaten us with my Da but my Da was soft with us although he was a brave man.

My Da was a seaman who served on *HMS Illustrious* during the war. Only young boys then. My Da served with Frank Agar's on HMS Illustrious.

HMS Illustrious

Boy and Man at Sea

I've been a seaman from the age of 17 then I was in the Queen Victoria Seaman's Rest in London for three years. That was our base.

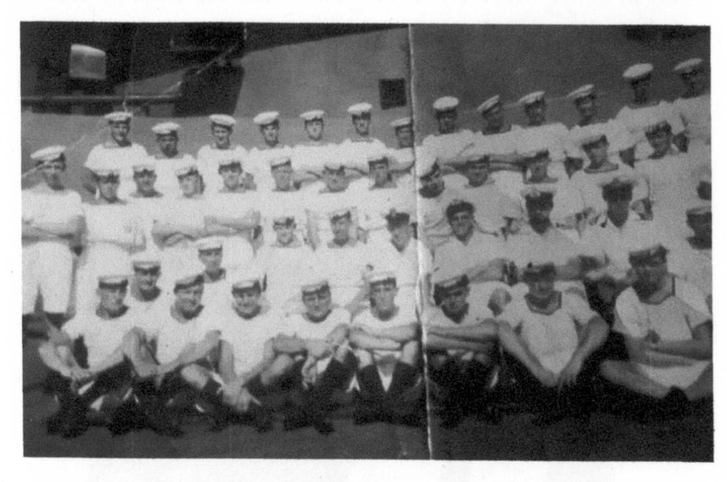

Then about 26 years ago I ended up in Hulme for my sins and have been kept here ever since, against my will of course!

I would give my life to go back to sea again! That will stay with me for the rest of my life. I was 17 and a half and I joined up in Liverpool. I joined up to the Norwegian merchant navy.

My first ship was the *Black Prince*, I was petrified, and I can still see the size of the waves, and then going down the bow it felt like hours, I was praying and praying for my life and I said I would never go again.

But coming back on land with pockets full of money I was desperate for a beer or a girl, whichever happened first. And you know it took a

Seaman's Rest

while for me to be able to walk on land again, it felt like the land was still moving beneath you, that's why sailors have that swagger.

There is no country on god's earth where there is water where I haven't been at least once over 15 years and 52 ships. I have met many of the Royals - this was Princess Alexandra...

Brian and Princess Alexandra

A Girl In Every Port And Gloria

This girl is some girl, she is called Gloria - I met this girl in Hong Kong and would you believe it, I was sat in a bar in Manchester and who pops up! She was even more beautiful in real life. I believe in coincidences - I think she will be there when I go up!

On Guard!

We took over the guards in Chelsea and the Queen used to drop in unannounced to inspect the horses, I told her "next time give us some warning, I'll make you a cup of tea!"

I guarded Rudolf Hess, Deputy Nazi Leader at the time he was arrested and Otto Adolf Eichmann, the infamous organiser of the Holocaust, in 1962/63 in Spandau Prison in Berlin. I was there when the wall was going up - there were four sections the French, British, American and German - to stop the Russians coming through.

Pubs In Hulme

I liked the pubs, it was like being home, everyone had jobs and your dad was a bad pig, you know. He used to sing to me "Liverpool Lou" and I used to tell him to cut it out.

There was a little clique and it was hard to get a start until Jimmy Kelly gave me a start, God rest his soul and I never stopped from then.

The Red, The Church and Clyne's or Woskys, as it was known, everybody just seemed to stay in these three pubs. If walls could talk hey!

Clyne's was my favourite place - singing in lock-in sat next to Jimmy Kelly, talking treason, the craic was mighty, drinking until we were mortified. I was singing one song and him another. Many happy days and nights were had in there.

Clyne's Bar

The Church Inn

The Red Admiral

Ahh here is me and Margaret Wilson, a great character; she was a stunning looking woman in her day, considered the Elizabeth Taylor of Hulme.

Hulme Now

Well it is certainly not the same, there is not the same craic now and all the pubs are shut!

On Top Of The World's next venture is a drama project devising a play with Hulme residents. This a previous play which gives you a taste of our next production.

THE HOPTON HOPEFULS
BY TINA CRIBBIN

Joe was holding court at the Salutation Pub. Long, loping and skinny when younger, he filled out a little in his mid-fifties, but lost it again once he hit 70. By that time, he refused to buy anything new and consequently his clothes of Autumnal shades, which were usually made of wool and corduroy, hung off him, highlighting his stoop and unsteady gait.

He still held the light in his eyes of devilment and hope of better things to come. Of respecting the need for and of having the craic and a pint. And of being a man's man. "Not like these soft arse young uns these days, sure they never knew a day's work".

Joe was surely a charmer. A bouncer back in the day, as well as a brickie, laborer, and bus driver. Storyteller, and pub jester, yeah you could say he was a legend.

The local students kept a wide berth but if some were feeling particularly brave they would use his catchphrase "go away and shite yourself" - to an innocent ear it sounded magical.

Joe: "Twas heartbreaking right enough the last of old Stig's gang all gone now, [deep sigh] that's the ways it goes I suppose.

"Even the buildings they made and the roads they laid are now smashed to bits. I walked past the only other pub left its half standing, a shell now. I stood outside having me roll up and as the wind changed direction I heard the voices, the laughter and the fights, I could smell the bitter, the fags and the sweat of the gangs from hardworking men. But the sadness struck me. I could feel that old pub aching with stories to tell and I could feel the loss bleeding from its half smashed bricks. It will be gone soon; just like us, there is nothing to say that we were on this earth, that we mattered that we gave our soul to this country. I'm tired of being invisible, tired of being a ghoul in my own home! The only thing left of us will be in a picture safely held behind glass and a cedar wood frame at some "real ale pub".

Enough now of the wallowing, time to fight back and what better way, than with the weasel's promise. He swallows hard and turns to Lacey his eyes bright with emotion.

Ballybough Joe: "Jay sus it was the business right enough though. Twas unlimited beer and shenanigans afoot! The best wake ever! I tell ya, what a way to go! I was dancing away there til early hours, grand it was! "

Lacey: "Aye, Is that right? Is it true he fell out of the window whilst trying to climb out of old Maggie's bedroom? You'd think he was a young fella", [*he laughs]*

Lacey began rubbing his hands together. Knuckles rough, his hands worn into shapeless pads from years of grafting, drinking, fighting and loving. A small portly man with bright ginger tuffs, and a face that didn't change with age. A sad looking face brought on from years as being described as the runt of the family. However what no one noticed was that his intelligence was bordering on genius, which he felt wasn't always a great thing. At times he wished he didn't see what was going on around him.

His redeeming quality wasn't his intelligence, it was the fact he was a champion Jiver in the Irish clubs of Manchester and now he still had a list of ladies who would give him a turn. Sometimes he braved it when he had the whisky chasers but he paid badly the next day. Despite his age as he said often "sure I'm not dead yet" he rebelled wearing his middle sons tracksuits and too big trainers. You couldn't miss Lacey.

Joe: "Well that man was a real ladies man right enough Jaysus any of the 13 kids that we know of would tell you that."

Lacey: "Aye, but Joe what about the dough? Did you hear anything?"

Joe: [*whispers]* "Well now I have a thing to tell you about that, so I have, get the word round 5 o clock to the Sally" *[he puts his long bony finger to his nose and gave a slow wink]* "Hold the whist now, off you go."

Lacey gave a quick nod and scampered off across Cambridge Street and into Hopton Court Tower block, or 'Ireland's Own' as it was sometimes called. It was a one of the last remaining buildings of the old Hulme refurbished in line with the student accommodation steel and smoked glass. Where you would find some of the old gang who made up a dysfunctional family of sorts.

With a glint in his eye and a spring in his step he had not felt since his last visit to Rosie of the road, he blushed slightly at the thought. She was a fine horse of a woman that one. The money! Finally the money!

The lift, although refurbished, at times still held the smell of yesterday's beer. He noted the camera eyeing him up, put his head down and stifled a grin. The Weasel had actually come through in the end. Ach sure he could never believe otherwise he was one of us after all when all's said and done.

Now to get hold of John Jo I hope he's not in with your old one, Myra. She's a walking serpent, and can read us all like a book.

Lacey knocked on John's flat but already knew the answer. If he was in you'd get a smile at the window as that's where he leaves his gnashers. Never leaves home without them, It was pointless trying to pass Myra's, she knew everything that happened on her watch. Her door sprung open like shed been waiting.

Myra "Is that you yourself young fella, come away in and tell me the news. John! In here!"

Myra was a living saint and demon depending if you crossed her. Her brain was as sharp as any 25 year-old for sure. Tower block mammy, everyone went to Myra for advice or just a sense of home.

She loved her pan stick and lippy and was always coordinated immaculately and there was always a handkerchief on hand if needed or not. Although often sporting legging and hoodies if going to Moss Side Leisure Centre for keep fit for those with COPD, most days Myra had some sort of sporty outfit on as she practiced her exercises at the window of her ground floor flat. You would often see Myra in mid exercise, her skinny leg posturing in mid-air. Much to the concern of the upstairs passengers on the 86 bus that went past her flat at ten-minute intervals. Myra would grin triumphantly at them, she was a marvel right enough! She was a small lean firecracker, with bright sparkling clear blue eyes.

INSIDE MYRA'S FLAT

Myra: "Now then John Jo it's the young fella Tommy Lacey calling for you".

Lacey: "Alright yourself John Jo"

John Jo: "Aye"

Lacey: Joe is looking at holding a meeting at the office about five [*he winked*] important business"

John Jo: "Aye Lacey to be sure important business you say, well we may need a few jars to discuss important matters I think"

Myra: "You do know this man's got diabetes, he can't be off gallivanting drinking and doing tomfoolery with you lot!"

Lacey: "Myra settle yourself down he's a grown man so..."

Myra: "You would do well for taking a leaf out of the judge's book; than going off to so call 'meetings'. Will ya give it up! The whole lot of you! You stupid heathen Ammadans! Not a brain between you all."

Lacey: "Sorry Myra it's just that we need this meeting you know I've been having problems with them pension's banjos, cos they say I have too many names getting paid on the lump all that time didn't do me any favours"

Myra: "Well right enough Jimmy" [*Judge Rinder's comes on the TV her and John Jo turn to TV interested]*

Myra: "Aw Jaysus no wonder he left! Look at her! A whore's melt if ever there was one. How many kids? Suffering Jaysus! God bless em and save them! And the mother still wearing leopard print and lipstick! Bad cess!"

Lacey: "Ach now Myra give her a chance she was left with seven kids to bring up she had to feed them somehow."

Myra: "May all the saints and our mother herself! Pray for that one talking dirty things on the phone*! [Myra blesses herself and John]* What is the world coming to."

John Jo: "Well now, that new fella of hers he's trying. Isn't he saying he wants them to move to a big house. "

Myra: "You big eejit with immoral earnings! Look at them eyes he's a shifty looking article right enough and his feet! I'll tell you never trust a man with small feet. He's pumping her out!"

Lacey: "Don't you mean pimping?"

Myra: "No I don't. I mean pumping! Every last hapenny out of her, the poor derelict sow. No! The judge although he is a bit you know, how's your father, but he has beautiful clean hands. Look not a hair out of place! A clever man, he will sort madam butterfly out right enough. Right then Jimmy the kettle calling you. And a bit of Pek on the table

Lacey: "Ah now then Myra I've just been having me lunch I'm grand thanks anyway."

Myra: "Have you've been drinking the potion? I went round the back of St Augustines for that."

Lacey: "Well now Myra here's the thing, I've felt like a new man ever since."

Myra: "Hmmm, well all you boy's big stinking beer bellies are still with ya, you may need an extra potion." [*Jimmy quickly goes out the front door]*

Lacey: "Bye then Myra"

Lacey breathed a sigh of relief. Where next he thought. Then he frowned when he realized: bloody porn tash Jimmy! On the seventh floor Jimmy had a variety of names such as Victor Meldew, Burt Reynolds and Porn Tash Jim to name a few.

Jimmy was 70 when you say hello to him, he would often greet you with a

snarl. He had the best 70s moustache, which he was very proud of. It still showed his virulence he thought. From the hard streets of Glasgow and from a family of eleven children Jimmy had become an adopted Irishman in Hopton which was earned over the years through hard drinking and crying at the lyrics of famous Irish songs.

AT JIMMY'S FLAT

Jimmy: "Lacey, the devil you want?"

Lacey: "Morning yerself you miserable auld goat" *They both smiled.* Joe is holding a meeting at the office five o clock, you there"

Jimmy: "No! They're all a bunch of auld Irish gits I've no interest in any of them!"

Lacey: "Ah so it's true, Jimmy you legend! You finally brought back Vulgaria, from Bulgaria!"

Jimmy: "Get away; she's my wee cleaner, Turn off the sky woman! You nae understand it!"

Vulgaria: "Pig head Jim you say we live in big house with big car and party! I not happy Jimmy!"

Jimmy: "What's up with you woman you've been to Wetherspoons on the bus. Now carry on in the kitchen."

Jimmy looked at Lacey and gave a shrug. The agreement had been made, he turned to say goodbye but before he got the chance the door was slammed in his face. Jimmy would be there. The shouting from the flat got louder....

Jimmy: "Vulgaria my darling I was only messing, c'mon here and give your man a wee cuddle."

Vulgaria: "Bad Jimmy! Are you sorry?"

Jimmy: "Aye Princess I'm wearing my best apron for you and the ovens warming nicely now."

Vulgaria: "Ok Jimmy, you know what happens if you make princess Vulgaria angry."

Lacey began sniggering his way to the lift to the last of them - Donegal Frank (hard as bacon shanks) as he was known. He lived in on the third floor Frank was the finest storyteller and best singer there was.

Donegal as he was known, he was notorious for being out in all weathers without a coat. He says his body acclimatized from working on the roads for years. As he says, real men don't need coats!

Donegal with his confirmation (two inches too short) pants his brown woolen jumper just about covering his beer belly that took a few decades to grow. Donegal was 80 years old but still had dark hair and had the face of a rascal that you couldn't help but warm to. He had the hands of a Navvy and a Celtic heart through and through. But he was his own worst enemy

AT DONEGAL'S FLAT

Lacey: "Donegal away your wanted."

Donegal: "Now then Lacey is that yourself?"

Lacey: "Aye, Ballybough Joe says the Sally at five."

Donegal: "The Sally you say? I'm not sure."

Lacey: "Well there's nowhere else what's up with you?"

Donegal: "Jimmy got barred after putting on Irish music and tapping the table."

Lacey: "Aw don't worry about that now sure. Do you remember the pubs Donegal do you?"

Donegal: "I miss them all! Fine, fine nights! Romancing, dancing and blaggarding - the laughs we had! Even the ones I didn't particularly like at least we had a community then. Jaysus! The university treat us as if we are already a bloody museum; A boring museum at that because no one ever comes to visit! I want to scream at them we are still here! Jaysus leave us a little something will ya! Sure we built half the buildings in Manchester."

Lacey: "But Donegal that's exactly why we have to stay put in the Salutation they took everything else - it's a war and we need to mark our territory! We have to keep fighting for all the fellas that are not here anymore. It's our tradition. Didn't we lot wake up to the signs 'no Irish, no blacks and no dogs' we got through that and if we stick together we can get through this. The boys last stand now. Our last stand lets enjoy it."

Donegal: "That pub holds all my memories, and the stories are in its walls there in the veins of the building. Sure, do you remember when Dillon was the landlord the summer outings? Waking up and gangs of men heading off for the summer outing still drunk from famous Dillon's lock in and poteen from the night before where they all slept where they fell. All of us big suntanned fellas who were hard as nails, and not a worry in the world, played hard, but worked even harder. That bar itself remains loyal to us Lacey. It knows its kin. It holds its doors open with a wide warm grin for us.

"I'm heart sore tired of them looking down their nose at me walking down the very streets me and my gang laid with our bare hands.

"I remember the day when I got my first job navvying. I was seventeen, I didn't look like much of a navy: all skin and bones in need of a good feed. But I took up that pick and went belting at it hell for leather! But for all that I didn't make a dint in that rock, I might as well stayed home. If it was not for a Kerry man showing me the ropes. I worked so hard I mean I couldn't have any of the lads saying what kind of man is that he can't work like a proper navvy? I had blisters on my hands and my back felt as if somebody had been laying about it with a stick, All I could think of was sending the postal order back home, and for what I didn't even get enough stamps for me pension.

"Right enough Lacey I'm in! Time to show them the boys are back in town!"

Lacey: "Aye Frank and I'm sure you could tell us a few more tales as well but I've got to be off now I'll see you at the Sali later."

Donegal: "Whilst you're here. Did I ever tell you about my casino? You see now here's the thing I was over in France and it just so happens I owned a casino. Well I was a big fella then; all the ladies loved me right enough. I had a boat, a Rolls Royce and a driver. But me being me I was still hankering after something. Anyways and anyhow this night, a fine looking man came in in a white suit with fine white hair and dark dark eyes with gold dripping off his hands and neck.

"He faced up to me, I could tell there was something amiss with this fella and sure enough, when I looked down I noticed he had the old shuffle going on and his feet look different somehow, encased in expensive alligator type shoes. Hmmm I says to me self, you're in for it now boyo. But I was young and foolish and I eyed the man right back. Well now Frank he says 'I heard you like a gamble tonight I'm going to gamble my wife… for your Casino…'

"My blood was pumping, and began pumping even more when looking at the wife. The blonde she was deadly! Tall, slim with bright green eyes, she had a rich look about her - classy. Sure she was heavenly! Her eyes were eating me alive.

"We sat round the table with the full moon giving the table and its occupants a strange eerie glow and we began to play. Well as the night wore on and the tension began to rise, I could see I was losing, I knew I was done for. It was the last set of cards and I put down two Jacks as the yoke began to put the cards on the table a big cloud passed over the moon and the whole place went deadly black, as black as black! Now then as the cloud began to pass and I heard a shuffling below I looked under the table and what do you think...The man had CLOVEN FEET! I was playing with the devil himself.

"Well now the cards fall on the table silently. I had lost but being a passionate man and a man of adventure I was thinking of the deadly blonde. I turned towards her with my best smile. She smiled back, life wasn't so bad but she left me quick enough and I found myself back in Manchester here in the Hopton Hilton living a poor man's life."

Lacey: "Frank save the next one till tonight! And make sure you line your stomach before you come out!"

THE SALUTATION PUB

Tucked into the corner of Higher Chapman Street between the Royal College of Music and MMU, students and lecturers sit in the Salutation Pub drinking real ale and debating, or worse playing board games. The boys would smile friendly at them all but between them they thought them strange. They welcomed everyone and didn't want to rock the boat as it was the last house standing.

Joe arrived first, he had a raging thirst on him. He was surprised and delighted to see an old familiar face at the bar. Sally Casey was a sight for sore eyes to any of the men in Hulme, there was something regal about the way Sally held herself, she was always turned out immaculately. She was a feisty, dainty lady but she only had good to say about everyone and you could always have a good laugh and chat with her. The boys will be delighted, he thought.

Joe: "Well then yourself Sally, it's grand to see you here like old times"

Sally: "Hiya Joe I'm just helping out in the summer whilst students are away, How are you Joe? Sorry to hear about the weasel passing, I know you were tight, it's a crying shame alright, we seem to be losing everyone."

Joe: "Aye Sally sure, but we've got to keep on going we're still here! Give me a drop of the black stuff will ya."

Sally: "Now Joe don't kid a kidder. On the house me laddo."

Joe: "Truth be told Sally I will miss him badly but the boys are on their way."

Sally: "Ah the seanchais! I hope the bar is stacked!"

The boys enter the pub

Frank: "Jaysus John Jo it was 1976 that you borrowed me that old rag and your still raging on about it!"

John Jo: "Well now that was the finest tweed, twas very expensive it came from Knock. My sister Mary had it blessed in the convent."

Frank: "That's why I never had any luck in it! You're always going on about money, Pogue muah ho-en!"

Lacey: "Never mind the suit it's a drink we are after, we are in a pub you loon."

Jimmy: "You two, you're like old ones arguing, away and get a pint. Look more students in here they're like rabbits!! Do you know you can only get a plot in Southern Cemetery if you're a student, they are literally robbing my grave!"

Lacey: "Ah go on now Jimmy you're having a laugh surely?"

Jimmy: "No, I tell you unless you got a student card you can't get buried in Manchester anymore, you have to be educated before you can die now for god's sake!"

Frank: "You can't be buried, married, or christened in the Holy Name anymore unless you are a student I know that's true."

Joe: "Settle yourself Jimmy it won't matter a dot when you're dead anyway!"

John Jo: (*walks to the bars and turn to Donegal waits silently*) "And another thing I didn't want to mention it but I'm still short of a bottom set of teeth."

Frank: "Jesus, Mary and Joseph give it up! Those teeth were lost in the Ardri in 1984. Some culchie knocked them right outta me. I was a great fighter back then."

Joe: "Right lads stop your messing we got business to deal with."

RESERVED TABLES

Lacey: "You may have a problem with that... look our usual table is reserved"

Frank: "Stop will ya! It's a pub not a restaurant, it can't be reserved"

John Jo: "It will be for those intellectuals I suppose"

Lacey: "What? They're so clever they need a reserved sign to show them where to drink?"

Joe: "Aye and a sat nav to tell them where the toilet is!"

Landlord: "Does there seem to be a problem, gentleman?"

Joe: "What's the crack with signs, we've been drinking here years there's never been reserved signs before"

Landlord: "Well times change and we now offer food"

Frank: "Food is it? Great I will have some bacon and cabbage and we'll just sit ourselves down nicely here"

Landlord: "Err it doesn't quite work like that and we haven't got any bacon or cabbage our special today is avocado fries with feta cheese and spinach parcels, with a dusting of crushed pine nuts"

Lacey: "Do I look like a starving rabbit wearing a peace badge? You're not feeding a load of virgin vegans now"

Landlord: "There's seating in the backroom if you wish to stay but this table is reserved"

Lacey goes to kick off but Joe intervenes

Joe: "C'mon now fellas settle yourselves remember we have bigger chips to fry than avocados, away and sit down"

The lads made their way to the back of the pub, but ensuring they make the landlord aware that this was a fight that wasn't finished.

John Jo: (*eyeing Sally at the bar)* "Would you look at that sight before me! How are you Sally? You've made my day right enough. Would you errr? Be having one yourself darling?"

Lacey: "John Jo you dark horse playing it smooth right enough!"

Joe: "Come away John and sit down. Okay, I declare this meeting officially open. Now say the oath."

Donegal: "But Joe we made that oath 40yrs ago when we were laying the A6. I know it's only said on serious occasions but I always feel a fool"

Joe "An oath is an oath my son!"

All: "We do solemnly swear to uphold the honour of the black stuff by laying as much as possible, drinking as much as possible and to understand that to spill it is a crime against the code. We promise to honour the code of the road and that whatever is said in the pub stays in the pub so help me god!"

Donegal: "What's that you got Joe?"

Joe: "It's the Weasel's promise."

Jimmy: "There's no money in that! He's having us on!"

Joe; "Do you remember the night lads! It was the weekend before Scotch week in Blackpool. That was a great night."

Joe: "He's right boys but like Jimmy I'm not holding my breath on a bet that was made 40 years ago."

John Jo: "Well the weasel was one of us, when all of us put our bonuses in on the table that night we said whoever wins will be trusted to put it all way till he passes. We all meant that didn't we?"

Jimmy looks uncomfortable Lacey starts looking at the window whistling

John Jo: "I did and rightly or wrongly I believed the man's word."

Lacey: "Aye but that article of a barmaid from the Red Admiral and himself went missing for two weeks straight after that promise, didn't his wife take the five kids up to Southport and left them there with them. He soon came back the kids in tow and his tail between his legs."

John Jo: "Surely that was just coincidence"

The lads all shook their heads at John Jo's innocence, it was one of the things they loved most about him.

Joe: "This calls for a whiskey chaser. Same again Sally with a Bells all round, Porntash is paying."

Jimmy: "You lot don't miss a trick I know it's my turn!"

Joe: "Right then this is it."

Sally came from round the bar to put the drinks down quickly. Joe put the letter down beside him. Sally sits next to him on the letter.

Sally: "Ah now then Joe you go easy, make sure these fellas here look after you, you need the boys around you at a time like this."

Joe: "Now don't be minding yourself I'll be grand. Sure my glass is always full."

Sally smiled and reached up to collect the empties Joe noticed the letter was stuck to the back of her skirt… He looks frantically round at the others, pleading with his eyes to do something. Sally walked off behind the bar taking the letter with her.

Joe: "Aw Jaysus we can't let her see what that letter was about! Someone needs to get it back and quick!"

Donegal: "Well now I vote John Jo, he's a gentleman she will never suspect!"

John Jo: "Bad cess to you Donegal, she's a lady I am not touching her there! No way! It's not the way I was brought up!"

Jimmy: "You load of old women I'm off to get that letter and give her bahookie a wee slap an away with the letter myself."

Joe: "What's a Bahookie!"

Jimmy: "Her arse you dumb shite"

The boys all laugh, Jimmy gets up from the table and makes his way to the bar.

Jimmy: "Here Sally will you help me with this I cannae work this new phone"

Sally: "Sure Jimmy pass it over"

Jimmy "I don't trust any woman with my phone, my Bulgarian wee darling gets jealous"

The boys laughing in the background

Jimmy: "Away an boil yer head you auld eejits"

Sally: "I don't want to be looking at anything illegal now Jimmy!"

Jimmy: "Nar man it's me kids sent this video. I need ya to show which buttons ta press"

Sally: "Jaysus Jimmy it's a mammy you'll be wanting next."

Sally walks around the bar next to him Jimmy winks at the boys who all look nervous.

Jimmy: "Here come closer"

Sally goes closer just at that moment Jimmy gives her a slap on her bottom and takes the letter and puts it behind him. Joe goes up and quickly puts it into his pocket.

Sally: "Now then Jimmy, bad cess to you. There's a line and you've crossed it! You little gobshite how dare you!"

Jimmy: "Aw hen I couldn't help me self. I'm sorry darling it was just a joke"

Sally: "Last warning Jimmy boy! Last warning! What the blazes are you boys up to tonight? You all look like your planning something which has got me worrying as the brains you have is as scarce as hen's teeth!"

Joe: "Now then Sally ignore him, c'mon have a drink yourself."

Sally: "Umm no thanks Joe but I'm watching you ugly buckets of snots any funny business and you're all out!"

Joe gets out the letter out.

Joe: "Well this is it boys the day of reckoning, let's see if he comes through." Didn't know me old mucker was into poetry. [*Joe reads*] 'Down in the bowels of the Salutation where the old potcheen was made, sat five ugly fellas looking for my grave, But because you're a load of old eejits, And as thick as a two headed drill bit, I placed it for safe keeping below three feet, In a space where a gang of my old muckers regularly meet."

Donegal: "What the hell is that!?"

Joe: "Jaysus the old get! ha ha!"

Jimmy bent down and tried to look under the seat.

Joe: "Jaysus if he had two brains he would be dangerous! Give it up Jimmy, stop acting the maggot we need a plan."

Donegal: "Where's he hid it? Is it underneath the floor?"

Jimmy: "It will be under our regular table. Yeah must have been in the 80s when they did the refurbishment in here. They spent thousands on it, to make it look exactly as it did when we had just come over. The weasel and Muldoons had the contract."

Joe: "We got to rip the seat out, and get them tiles up. Who has any tools?"

Jimmy: "I know, Scouse Brian! He's got his fingers in all the pies. We are going to need a pneumatic drill to get through them tiles."

John Jo: "Now lads be careful, I don't want to be involved in anything not strictly legal, not at my age."

Donegal: "Go away man, sure nobody will know we will put all back no one will be any the wiser."

John Jo: "But the ages of us! Jaysus there's about four hundred years between us all. Are we able for it?"

Joe: "Well I'll tell you something for nothing, I'm fit as a fiddle I have not been to the docs for about twenty years sure. Look at these bad boys (*showing his arm muscles*) but we need to get the keys off Sally so we can come back tonight."

Lacey: "How are we going to manage that."

Joe: (*Looks at Jon Jo)* "Well who she thinks is the most innocent amongst us all?"

John Jo: "Now here I'm not sure now my old ticker is playing up I wouldn't know what to do."

Jimmy: "Ah go and hump off will ya. You don't have to do anything just keep your Beour talking while we get the keys near closing time."

Donegal: "I would love the chance to do some smooth talking with Sally but she would see right through me, she is a fine looking woman."

The evening wears on: Scouse Brian enters the pub complete with mobility scooter

Brian: "Alright Lads what's the score"

Joe: "Ah me mucker, c'mon over here and bring your thinking cap."

Brian: "Alright Joe not seen you since the wake, you seemed to be having some fun with that Edna woman."

Joe: "Wisht now Brian not such a thing at all at all"

Brian: "Alright lad, how can I help?"

Joe: "Read old Weasel's note and see if you can help us out."

Brian: "The man's a legend, la. You need tools. When do you need the gear for?"

Joe: "We've only got one chance of this and that's tonight".

Brian: "Well in honour of the old Weasel and the fact I'm always up for a bit of fun, give me a couple of hours, but count me in as well."

Joe: "No near closing time is better we're having a lock in, shh now."

Brian: "Enough said, lad."

Jimmy: "C'mon me laddie get over there and work your magic John Jo we're waiting on you son, so we are"

SALLY AND JOHN JO

John Jo: "Hiya Sally a pint of black and one for yourself."

Sally: "Aw bless you John I will, how are you keeping?"

John Jo: "Well now Sally truth be told I've been awful lonesome recently."

Sally: "Now then John Jo, a big fella like yourself you would have half the estate after you."

John Jo: "Stop will ya Sally, there's no one as lovely as yourself sure I've had the glad eye for you for many a year and I'm heart sore just thinking about you I am."

Sally: "Don't be blagarding me I'm too long in the tooth now. I will knock you to blazes I will."

John Jo: "I er I er loved you from afar Sally you know that."

Just then Jimmy crept up behind the bar and gave John Jo the eye.

Sally: "Now John Jo I'm a God-fearing woman. What would I want to be doing with a man? Not only that John Jo you're always off gallivanting. I would never get to see you."

John Jo: "But Sally I'm in the bed on my own every night.."

Sally began laughing at John Jo and she was going to turn where Jimmy was reaching for the keys. Jimmy eyed him urgently. Just then John Jo leaned over to Sally for a kiss on the cheek, but his lack of confidence got the better of him. Sally turned quickly her and John Jo's heads collided. Sally looked angry and confused.

Sally: "What the devil's up with you tonight, John? Are you ailing for something, is that it? Well I tell ya! You're ailing for a hiding all the way out the door so you are!"

John Jo: (*mumbling red faced*) "I'm terribly sorry I'm not sure what's happening today. Sorry"

Joe: "Quick now Jimmy, get them keys copied from Brady, he owes me a favour. I need them back in less than an hour."

Jimmy: "Who am I a wee lassie? Nar man I'm having my pint."

Lacey: "Err Jimmy are you busy with something or someone else from Bulgaria perhaps?"

Jimmy: "Ok I'm away I'm away! [*He slams his drink down in a huff and goes out*]

THE SALUTATION: JULY 1970

The pub is crowded with regulars and road gangs. Staff from Duncan and Fosters and Dunlops are smoking, laughing and shouting - all men

Music:

Brendan Shine : Do You Want Your Old Lobby Washed Down

Irish Rovers: Finnegans Wake

Danny Doyle: Green Hills of Killkenny

Dubliners: Whisky in the Jar

Dubliners: Seven Drunken Nights

John Jo: "Alright there fella you having one?"

Joe: "Is the Pope Catholic?"

John Jo: "Hiya Sally looking grand tonight. Are you sure you don't want to leave your husband and kids and run away with me."

Sally: "And where would you be taking me this time?"

John Jo: "You know Sally, that song."

Sally: "What's song that then?"

John Jo: "The three steps to heaven."

The bar erupts into laughter, John slinks away. Just then Lilly arrives and all the fellas turn.

Joe: "Here's my cheque Sal, can you change it?"

Sally: "Yes after lock up, you know the score. There's a couple of jars going round for Mickey Murphy's Mrs. and Kelly's trip home. It was an awful shame - two brothers killed outright in farming accidents. It doesn't bear thinking of."

Joe: "How's he holding up?"

Sally: "He's staying with Maggie for a bit she will keep an eye out for him and make sure he's able right enough."

Joe: "Just take fifty of my wages, there for the grace of god."

Sally: "Well we have to look after our own, speaking of which the meat man's in and Malone is looking for diggers in the Oldbury work camp."

Joe: "Is he now? That camp holds 20,000 men. It's not bad. They have their own pub, church and cinema, you could make a fair few bob."

Sally: "But surely you get lonely Joe?"

Joe: "I'm a long distance and Sally we're Irish isn't it our blood the leaving? The uprooting. It's an ache we know well and it's not just the menfolk either."

Lilly: (*Turns to Frank)* "All right cowboy a cherry B darling"

Frank: "Ah Lilly yes sure, how you keeping?"

Lilly: "I'm great you remembered that we were meeting tonight."

Frank: "Of course Lil, as if I would forget stepping out with a beauty such as yourself."

Lilly: "Now you know it's only a bit of company, no funny business. I'm a widow and you know I cherish the very ground my old fellas buried in. He was known as the rat of Rathmines. My mother God bless her, just called him a derelict drunk."

Frank: "Now now just enjoy yourself do you want another drink?"

Lilly: "Your skinny malink friend over there is already giving us the glad eye."

<u>**Weasel:**</u> "Hello doll, looking grand girl, that top of yours it's making me go blind"

<u>**Lilly**</u>: "I can make you go blind from something else."

<u>**Weasel**</u>: "Really!"

<u>**Lilly**</u>: "This fist in your face! Now get lost!"

<u>**Weasel:**</u> "There's something really sexy about a woman who has fire in her belly and a serpent's tongue."

<u>**Joe**</u>: (*laughing*) "You're a glutton for punishment boyo."

The night wears on…

<u>**Lilly and Frank**</u>: (*singing drunkenly leaning in to each other*) "Bang Bang Rosie Rosie bangs all day who's going to bang for Rosie when Rosie's gone away."

<u>**Frank:**</u> "There's a queer smell coming off you now Lilly what have you been doing?"

<u>**Lilly:**</u> "Well no one can say I'm not a good mother Frank, I've been shopping, I've got me meat wrap from Colin and I got a lovely selection of seafood from the cockle man."

<u>**Frank:**</u> "It smells like you're wearing them Lil"

Just then the cockle man walks past carry his basket, he smiles at Lilly and gives her a lazy wink.

<u>**Lilly**</u>: "Well you're not doing a body search that's for sure"

<u>**Frank:**</u> "C'mon now Lil let me just check for evidence. I think you may have lost a prawn or two."

THE WEASEL'S PROMISE

Weasel at a table drunk and maudlin speaking to old Murphy.

<u>**Weasel:**</u> "I remember journeys on the Princess Maud hundreds and hundreds of us coming across the water... cattle class. It's only 60miles but it might as well been 60,000. It was like a religious pilgrimage, all young boys hurt of the leaving, trying to be brave and forget about it, drinking and thinking ah its only for a little while. But that little while can last a lifetime. All the promises you made to yourself and family. What can I be saying. I spent my time in camps that you wouldn't let a dead dog lay in. Dogged by the Subby

and the pacemaker keep digging keep digging! Ah sure, I've jumped from the frying pan into the fire.

"Well the American dream is life liberty and freedom, the Irish version goes work drudgery and sweet FA. Digging the hole or pulling the cable, my life summed up. But no I won't put the pain to those back home. I just say the craic was mighty."

He gets up looking for a fight.

Lacey: "Frank Frank! C'mon there's a mighty row in the big room the Weasel's at it again"

Weasel: "I will after knocking the shite outta you all! I can take ten men! Me and my road gang can take the lotta you right here right now."

Lacey: "Who are you're fighting Weasel, there's no one there, man."

Donegal: "Leave him Lacey, show respect man - he's our gaffer if he says it's true it is."

Joe walks over to the weasel, trying to calm him down.

Joe: "C'mon now let's have a drink."

Weasel: "I love all you men like my brothers we have been on the road years but I'm getting on now boys, what will happen to us all where will we go?"

John Jo "Not at all, not at all. Your okay you're with us now."

Weasel "I am but I worry about you boys - none of us has insurance."

Donegal: "You're happy tonight Weasel, you've been on the Bells"

Weasel: "Who will look after you when I'm gone?"

John Jo: "You're going nowhere, it's the drink talking."

Lacey: "C'mon now weasel let's have a wager"

Weasel: "Aye a wager you say how about something a bit different."

Joe: "What's that you old goat"

Weasel: "Let all the gang put your bonuses in the tin for safe keeping and whoever goes first leaves it for the rest. At least that way whoever goes is sure to get a great send off"

Lacey: "Happy days hey! No way!"

Joe: "He's got a point sure we are on a load of green stuff from the Millgate brothers, we'll be grand."

Donegal: "How old is everybody then?"

Lacey: "Get lost Donegal you sound like the social I'm not going anywhere yet apart from the bar."

Joe: "Ok lads put your money in and your name in my cap whose name comes out first will be the holder of our fortune. Remember I said holder not spender!"

PRESENT DAY SALUTATION

Jimmy has returned with the copied keys, Scouse Brian is out the back with his tools and the boys are saying goodnight.

Joe: "Bye Sally, you get yourself away now. Do you want us to walk you over?"

Sally: "No boys I'll be grand just get away yourselves now, goodnight."

The boys make off slowly towards Hopton but turn down a side street which takes them to the back of the Salutation - hiding behind parked cars they watch Sally leave.

Scouse Brian: "It's been a while lads since we played out this late. Are we game on?"

John Jo: "I better be going now lads Myra will be on the warpath."

Donegal:" Are you a man or a mouse! Get yourself over here!"

Jimmy: "I tell you, no woman would be telling me what to do! My one is chained to the sink."

Lacey: [*smirking*] "Is that right Jimmy, Would that be Vulgaria then?"

John Jo and Joe: "What?"

Lacey: "Saw her with my own eyes this afternoon, Miss Bulgaria I was beginning to think she was an imaginary friend, deadly tattoos."

Jimmy: "Shut up Lacey, you know nothing she's just cleaning for me".

Lacey: "Is that right? Is that why you were wearing a frilly apron when you opened the door?"

Jimmy: [*getting up close and eyeballing Lacey*] "Listen you wee ginger nugget!

Lacey: "I still have it, I dance like a leprechaun and still sting like fin Mccool!"

Lacey tries to throw a punch but completely misses. Jimmy and Lacey start taking off jackets and rolling up sleeves but Lacey isn't wearing his glasses and keeps veering to the left. Donegal and Brian are roaring laughing and John Jo looks worried. Joe goes over and separates them.

Joe: "Listen you pair of eejits c'mon we got a job to do grow up. Jaysus the pair of you"

Brian and Donegal give another burst of laughter but stop when Joe gives them the look.

INSIDE THE SALI

Joe: "Sh, sh quietly now, Lacey go round the back and let Brian in with his scooter. Donegal, make sure all the curtains are closed."

Donegal: "Ok Joe."

Joe: "John Jo, see if you can dismantle that bench ,see if we can get under there."

Brian and Lacey come through and begin unloading the tools, John Jo is on the floor underneath the seat.

John Jo: "Sure, which eejit put this together; get me the best tool for the job - a hammer I'll have this walloped out in no time at all."

Joe: "Careful now we have to put it back the way it was."

John Jo: "Sure it will be right as rain."

Lacey passes him a hammer and he begins tapping underneath the seat then pulling on the supporting leg. Eventually it gives way and the boys lift the seat off. John Jo who's still on the floor, tries to get up

John Jo: "Arrghh my back my back!"

Donegal: "Shh now we'll be getting you up."

Lacey: "Jesus Mary and Joseph c'mon lads!"

They all lift John Jo who is covered in dust, he looks pale and they sit him on the seat facing.

Joe: "More power to your elbow you still got it!"

__John Jo:__ [*smiling now*] "Ach sure it was nothing but thirsty work right enough."

__Joe:__ "Later boys, let's get this thing out."

__Jimmy__: "Look, there's a hole in the floor there behind where the back supporting panel was, bad workmanship that."

__All:__ "An English man!"

__Joe__: "So there is Jimmy! Reach in and have a look will ya."

Jimmy reaches in and brings out a an old round biscuit tin

__Jimmy:__ "It's got some weight lads!"

All the boys are smiling and rubbing their hands.

__Joe:__ "Let's put that bench back before we do anything. Once we have a drink we won't be fit for anything."

__John Jo:__ "Not me Joe, I've an awful pain so I have."

__Jimmy:__ "A scotch man never gives up!" *He bends downs and asks Lacey to pass him some tools.*

__John Jo:__ "Did you ever do any building work before Jimmy?"

__Jimmy:__ "Away yourself"

The bench is cobbled back together and the boys are now sat around the center table with a bottle of whisky and the tin taking center stage. Joe begins to slowly take the lid off the tin.

__Joe:__ "Well now would you look at that!"

Notes are stuffed haphazardly in the tin around a big lump of tar. Next to an old medicine bottle.

__Donegal:__ "Jaysus! we're rich right enough."

__Joe:__ "Hang on there's a note here as well (*He reads from a crumpled bit of paper*). 'Enjoy lads the inks still wet!' What the hell?"

__Scouse Brian__: *lifting one of the notes up to the light laughing* "I'll tell you lads these notes are as bent as a nine bob note."

__Lacey:__ "No they look fine to me, a ten pound note"

__Scouse Brian:__ "Look on the back"

<u>**Lacey:**</u> *On the back was printed one pound note* "Bad Cess to him! And the curse of a thousand maggots be on his grave. Curse a god on you altogether Weasel!"

<u>**Donegal:**</u> "Let me see, let me see now. Aww Jaysus he's only fiddled us, I always knew he would the old dry shite."

<u>**John Jo:**</u> "Smiling well no good will come from no good. Jaysus ten on one side and a pound on the other! Ha Ha."

<u>**Jimmy:**</u> "And they call the Scotch tight! Away and drink we've earned it."

<u>**Joe:**</u> "He's right let's go to the bar."

<u>**John Jo**</u>: "I'm not stealing from the bar!"

<u>**Jimmy:**</u> "You're not, I am and it's from the University who has robbed our whole community of a life as we know it. Sure tis only the ghosts drinking we are invisible to them and they can afford a bottle of Bells Whisky suffering Jesus."

<u>**Donegal:**</u> "Well said Boyo well said! And may the Weasel's obituary be written in pig's piss.

<u>TWO HOURS LATER: ALL DRUNK</u>

<u>**Lacey:**</u> "Aye we had some grand times with the old Weasel didn't we boys."

<u>**John Jo**</u>: "A grand fella all together he was"

<u>**Donegal**</u>: "Aye a living saint."

<u>**Jimmy**</u>: "My Vulgaria she is a living saint, a goddess."

<u>**Joe**</u>: "Don't be swearing now man, we are remembering the dead."

<u>**Jimmy**</u>: "I'm not, that's her name. My wee darling so she is. Ah she makes me a better man."

<u>**Joe:**</u> "Are we going to do something about Brian?"

<u>**Donegal**</u>: "Ah sure he's grand now snoring away there in his carriage there so he is."

The boys begin singing, I'll take you home Kathleen. Suddenly the lights come on. At the door way are Sally, Myra and Vulgaria - all looking very angry!

<u>**Sally:**</u> "Having a good time are we boys?"

Joe: "Err we found the door open and we were protecting the pub for you, you know what it'is like round here."

Sally: "I do indeed. And were you protecting the bottles of Bells as well?"

Donegal: "No err we found the bottle like that."

Sally: "Just like that you found it in the bottom of your bellies your all derelict drunk!"

Myra: "John Jo Sullivan! What do you have to be saying for yourself! And look at the state of you! A good Catholic boy like you. I bet these eejits forced you didn't they John Jo?"

John Jo: "Myra, I've been trying to get away home for hours"

Jimmy: "Shut up you big Eejit you're the one who planned it."

Sally: (*Coming to the table and looking at the notes*) So the Weasel came through I could of told you not to bother. I've had his Mrs at mine crying over the same monopoly money. Jaysus not a brain cell between the lot of you."

Vulgaria: "Jimmy, you say we marry have big house and car with this money!"

Jimmy: "Ah darling I'm just not the marrying kind, lass and we can't now I've been conned out of the money."

Vulgaria starts crying Sally and Myra comfort her. Myra looks at Jimmy

Myra: "You rotten swine! May the curse of Mary Malone and all of her nine blind illegitimate children chase you so far over the hills of damnation that the Lord himself can't find you with a telescope!"

Jimmy: "That's a bit harsh now Myra."

Myra: "May you marry a wench that blows wind like a stone from a sling."

Sally: "Right that's it, your all barred! Barred the lot of you! Get away home now I've got to clean this place up!"

Donegal: "Sally is there's no chance of you putting on a couple of rashers?"

Sally: "OUT OUT!"

THE NEXT DAY

The boys sit around a table.

Joe: "I still can't believe that old toad."

John Jo: "Well now he left us something better than money"

Jimmy: "Yes nothing! Vulgaria was back on the plane the next day!"

Donegal: "Jimmy she was all over you like a rash then left you like a bad dose of the runs."

Jimmy: "Well she took off fast enough before the word skint even left me mouth. But nothing can change my mind, I love that woman, she made me a nicer person I'm going over there to marry her. As soon as I get my flight money."

All the boys laugh when he says she makes me a nicer person.

Joe: "We all look like a bunch of fools and Sally has just allowed us back in and them bloody students sat in our seats! Would you look at the shower of them their playing with building bricks what's the world coming to?"

Donegal: "What's happened to Lacey?"

Jimmy: "No doubt onto the next blag."

(Lacey comes swaggering in in looking like a student. He is wearing a Stone Roses hat, a tie-dye T-shirt, John Lennon glasses and ripped jeans complete with a parka and rucksack. The boys don't initially recognize him)

Lacey: "Hi would it be possible to get a pint of bitter in this establishment."

The barman: "Yeah certainly"

Lacey: "I've got a University ID. I'm the new professor there and err I'd like to reserve a table for 5 for approximately the next three months as part of the research I'm conducting. [*He gets a crumpled bit of paper out and starts to read*] I'm teaching the next intake of students on the development and refinery of Guinness in a working class Culture. Let me introduce myself. I am Amadeus Rupert Rafferty I originally taught in the University of Cork."

(The Barman looks closely at the card and shakes his head and gets the reservation book out. Lacey goes over to the table)

Jimmy: "What's the outfit? Who dressed you? *(Donegal and the boys laughing* *into their beer)*

Lacey: "Knock off Paul from number 25."

Jimmy: "You can tell. How did you know all the big words, you bollix?"

Lacey: "Well the Sullivan boy is a very learned man. The priests in Cork you know educated him. It's a script I have."

The boys snigger

Lacey: "You Langers you won't be laughing in a minute. I've only struck gold shh keep the noise down."

He brings out the student I.D cards just needing photos

Donegal: "There's nothing between them ears but a pickled brain!"

Lacey: "Well I'm teaching a degree about Guinness."

John Jo: "Fair play to you right enough." (*all the boys nod in agreement*)

Jimmy: "No one understands a pint like him from here to Donegal."

Joe: "Jesus Lacey how did you manage that?"

Lacey: "Knock off Paul has a load of magic machines in his flat. I told our situation he said he's a red."

John Jo: "You mean a United fan."

Lacey: "No he said he's a Communist. Had all weird things on the wall. I said 'I don't care what you do in private in your spare time it's a free country.'"

Donegal "Fair play to the lad."

Lacey: "He said you can go to him later and he'll sort your picture out. Now then here are the cards pick a name."

Jimmy "Look at the state of them names! Edmund, Bartholomew Godfrey and Tarquin!"

John Jo: "Myra will kill me if she hears I have a new name."

Lacey: "We can go anywhere with these. Just think Jimmy you can sort your plot out at Southern Cemetery now you miserable old get."

Jimmy: "I'm not having bleeding Tarquin on my headstone that's for sure."

Just then the boys hear a commotion and a creaking and the bench gives way. Students fall on the floor. The boys fall about laughing.

Donegal: "Never ask a Scotch man to build!"

Joe: "It's been the best bit of building I've seen in a long time!"

John Jo: "I told you he left us something better than money. A grand old tale and you can't put a price on that! Boys!"

The boys sit back and take in the commotion with huge smiles on their faces. Until the landlord comes back looking furious

Landlord: "You lot I might of known!"

Joe: "That has nothing to do with us now."

Landlord "Your bad building days are long over, I am talking about fraud!"

Lacey [*splutters into his pint]* "I've never done a bad day's building in my life!"

Landlord: "Well you're certainly not very good at forging documents, I had my suspicions and checked, Professor of Guinness. Ingenious simply ingenious except it isn't - you are all barred. Really gentlemen it's time to refrain from using this establishment. We have a certain clientele and an emerging reputation as one of the best handcrafted eateries in the area."

Jimmy: "It's a pub!"

Landlord: "That's what you gentlemen don't understand - it's an eating and social experience."

Jimmy: "It's a pub with fancy prices."

Landlord: "This is not getting us anywhere, kindly leave this establishment."

Donegal: "Well I have been thrown out of better places than this. But I am not wasting my pint."

Landlord: "Look I'm concerned about your health you really drink too much I noticed that you only buy two pints at a time."

Donegal: "Well you can't fly with only one wing!"

Landlord: "You are not listening leave! Now!"

Just then a young man appears beside them dressed in a suit. He looks familiar to Joe but he can't seem to place him.

Brendan "It's okayNick I will take it from here."

The landlord walks off clearly frustrated

Brendan "Well I have had a very interesting conversation with the landlord about a Guinness professor."

Lacey: "You can see that man's got problems"

Joe: "Who are you son?"

Brendan: "Sorry my name is Brendan Finn I run the writing school in the English department."

Joe: "Finn you say? No relation to Michael Finn and Dolores from Kilfernore?"

Brendan: "Yes they're my grandparents! How in the world!"

Joe: "Sure I played with your grandfather as a child."

Brendan: "I am amazed2

Joe: "Ah not at all we know our own. So you're a Paddy then?"

Brendan: "I was born in Manchester."

Joe: "You're a paddy, so what's the craic Brendan can you help us out?"

Brendan "I'm sure it's fate but before I had that phone call I was in a meeting with the Dean and we were putting together a new course of writing which includes oral storytelling to allow our students to have a richer experience. My proposal included storytelling nights here examining our oral heritage. Would you gentleman be interested - we could pay you a small fee per session."

John: "Now here I'm not doing anything mucky mister!"

Brendan: "No it's just sitting here and have students come and listen to your stories."

Joe: "A fee you say, would that involve lubrication?"

Brendan: "It's up to you what you spend it on."

Lacey: "Would we be considered students?"

Brendan: "No but your place of work would be here so you would have to be here twice a week in term time."

Lacey [*smiling and rubbing his hands]* "Well that sounds reasonable."

Donegal: "I'm not sure I have anything to talk about."

All the boys fall apart laughing

Brendan: "If you're anything like my grandad you do."

Joe: "Sure enough we can put a few old tales together."

John: "So is it like a proper job? What would we be called?"

Brendan: "Well I suppose your title would be An Oral History Consultant."

Lacey: "Wow! We'd have to get a suit and everything for that."

Donegal: "I've still got the tweed one from Mulvaneys wake in '86 though it's a bit tight."

Brendan: "No gentlemen come exactly as you are."

Jimmy: "Is this the real deal? I don't like talking to people will just help out going to the bar."

Brendan: "So you will be their P.A, their personal assistant."

Joe: "And whose money would you go to the bar with Jimmy?"

Jimmy: "Well not my own I'm saving for me wedding, I'll do anything."

Brendan: "Let's start next week and see how it goes."

Joe: "Does this mean we're not barred?"

Brendan: "Exactly gentlemen I will have a word with the Landlord."

Brendan speaks to the landlord who is red in the face and gestulating. His body language eventually shows a reluctant agreement. He comes over with drinks.

Landlord: "Now gentlemen we may have got off on the wrong foot I didn't realize you were involved in the creative industries. I am looking forward to the storytelling night, it will give this pub such authenticity."

John: "Thank you."

Jimmy: "Okay leave us be now we will just finish our pints in peace."

Joe [*smiling]* "Well boys can you believe that their's life in the old dogs yet! And if it's a story their after it's a stories they will get. Sure aren't we one of them now."

Jimmy: "We will never be one of them but we can educate them!"

Donegal: "Ah it will be a great night!"

Joe: "A toast to the Seanchais."

THE NIGHT OF STORYTELLING

In the pub, all the guys have dressed up and are nervously waiting near the bar.

Joe: "Jimmy what are you doing with that book? You know what I drink."

Jimmy: "This is my Filofax it's needed for all your appointments."

Joe: "What appointments?"

Jimmy: "The Irish center have been asking for a night and some bar in Chorlton you're gonna be famous lads! If it keeps up like this I will be married in less than six months. Me and Vulgaria are skypeing again."

The boys all laugh

Brendan: "Right lads are you ready?"

There's a round of applause from the crowd of students and professors

Brendan: "I would like to introduce a group of heritage heroes who have some compelling tales to tell but let's begin with why are these tales so important, why are they important now?

Joe stands up nervously towards the mike.

FINAL MONOLOGUE

Joe: "It's important because of the Princess Maud, because of the leaving. Because of the loss. Because all our lives we were under estimated. Because of the famine and the bog, because of the pain behind Donegal's rheumy eyes when he talks of "home" because we never had a chance to be boys. Because our mothers died a little each time one of her boys said he was going foreign across the water. And we watched her grow smaller with her hand to her mouth holding in her cries of pain.

"Because of the hurt, because of the signs which said 'no blacks no dogs no Irish' because our heritage is of joy and loss. Because I can't un see, I feel every hurt and heartbeat. Because we know our own.

"Because we were forced into uprooting and leaving of our homes, our way back, travelling cattle class to England. Or staying at home with no work no food, while everyone knew you were able to provide. If you only went across the water. Man up Boyo Man up!

"And still you were blamed for the leaving. And still blamed for the staying. The only time it eases. Is when you're sat with your own talking and joking and laughing and laughing about anything else but that.

"Because our storytelling covers a pain we're not allowed to talk about. So we find a 'home' of sorts in the pubs in Hulme. Where men were men, and deals were made, business and partnerships grew, where we spent night after night after working twelve hours on the road. Where men with big calloused hands held mountains of money, which came from behind the bar and most of it was spent back, or it was squirreled away for your sister's wedding dress or the child's communion.

"We were paid on the lump, most of us didn't have bank accounts. It's where you would get your next job, room, or house, it's where you found news from back home of the living and those whose passed. It's where a jar would be passed round to pay for Duffy's funeral or help towards his kids; it's where you arrange to visit the sick and lend a hand to some family that's moving, it's where you find the peacekeeper to sort out the arguing in the work gangs or seek marriage guidance.

"It's where you found friends, which had become family. It's where you left to go on a Charrabanc to Blackpool or Southport where the only sounds on the bus was the opening of cans and weary sighs as hard men gave their bruised and aching backs a day off.

"It's where you're not the only one who cries for the longing of home in old Irish tunes and at the same time cursing the country to hell. It's where you describe your pain as unbearable solid black mass and the next fella knows his so well he has given his a name. It's being a misfit but fitting in. It's where you're accepted, it's where you find kin. It's the heartbeat of community and it's where you became a man.

"Times good and bad passed, and the tales grew within the walls of the pub which was a vessel of dreams and longing of us and the other men who drank there. As we got older it became more of a Community Centre different drinking times, same old craic watching the seasons and fashion change through the smoky windows supping a pint next to the racing times, still happy and content.

"Then we noticed the buildings disappearing but we're not working and we feel invisible to all the workers, as they banter amongst themselves. We no longer have a role, our friends began dying and the only social gathering is at the latest wake and there have been many.

"The development is so fast it's hard to know where you are. The roads have all changed, and the families leave and the shops close, all the other pubs close, and we are left... left with a few of our own like ourselves who can't face the pain of the leaving again. Those pub walls - hold them as tight as a mother's love. We are not prepared to leave so easily. Because we have already spent a lifetime in pain,

"Because that feeling of difference runs hot through your veins and fills you up until it has nowhere else to go. But despite that and because of that you need to come closer and see the light behind our eyes. There is the most beautiful light if you only stopped and looked."

Donegal gets up. Joe sits down and the audience is quiet and shocked. But then it starts with a slow clap and builds into steady applause.

Donegal: "Hush now! Did I ever tell you about the casino I had in France?"

The boys erupt laughing and Joe stands proudly watching the night unfold.

Ends with the Dubliners 1977 McAlpine's Fusiliers song.